WRITING FANTASY & SCIENCE FICTION

and getting published

Brian Stableford

TEACH YOURSELF BOOKS

Long renowned as the authoritative source for self-guided learning – with more than 30 million copies sold worldwide – the *Teach Yourself* series includes over 200 titles in the fields of languages, crafts, hobbies, sports, and other leisure activities.

A catalogue record for this title is available from The British Library

Library of Congress Catalog Card Number: on file

First published in UK 1997 by Hodder Headline Plc, 338 Euston Road, London NW1 3BH

First published in US 1998 by NTC Publishing Group
An imprint of NTC/Contemporary Publishing Company
4255 West Touhy Avenue, Lincolnwood (Chicago), Illinois 60646·1975 U.S.A.

The 'Teach Yourself' name and logo are registered trade marks of Hodder & Stoughton Ltd in the UK.

Typeset by Hart McLeod, Cambridge.

Printed in England by Cox & Wyman Limited, Reading, Berkshire.

Impression number 10 9 8 7 6 5 4 3 2 1
Year   2000 1999 1998 1997

808.3876
STAB

CONTENTS

ACKNOWLEDGEMENTS

I am indebted to the students who have taken my various courses in creative writing, whose relentless demands for enlightenment have helped me to formulate the answers set out herein. I am particularly indebted to Martin Akehurst, Alison Brecknell, Louise Manuel, Evelyn Ryle and Penny Williams, who read parts of the text while it was in progress and offered useful criticism. I am also indebted to my wife Jane, who proofread the penultimate draft and made many helpful suggestions.

ABOUT THE AUTHOR

Brian Stableford was born in Shipley, Yorkshire in 1948 and was educated at Manchester Grammar School and the University of York. He lives with his wife and an enormous collection of books in Reading, his two children having grown up. He lectured in sociology at the University of Reading before becoming a full-time writer in 1989, although he continues to teach an extra-mural class on "Writing Fiction". He has published more than forty science fiction and fantasy novels, including *The Empire of Fear*, *Young Blood* and *The Hunger and Ecstasy of Vampires*, and more than a hundred short stories, some of which are collected in *Sexual Chemistry: Sardonic Tales of the Genetic Revolution*. He is a prolific writer of non-fiction about the history of imaginative fiction and is a major contributor to *The Encyclopedia of Science Fiction*, *The Encyclopedia of Fantasy*, *The St James Guide to Fantasy Writers* and the forthcoming *St James Guide to Horror, Ghost and Gothic Writers*. He is a recipient of the Distinguished Scholarship Award of the International Association for the Fantastic in the Arts and the Science Fiction Research Association's Pioneer Award. He is also the editor of several anthologies, including *The Dedalus Book of British Fantasy* and two *Dedalus Books of Decadence*.

1
FALLING SPARROWS: WORLDS WITHIN TEXTS

The scope of this book

The purpose of this book is to help you to write fantasy and science fiction stories. As the title admits, writing is something you have to teach yourself, by practising long and hard, but I hope this book will help you to practise more effectively. I shall try to achieve that by making you more aware of what you are doing when you write, enabling you to examine the inner workings of your stories and plan their construction more carefully.

Readers do not, of course, dissect stories in this way. Although they could, if asked, describe the characters or summarise the plot of a story they have read, they do not analyse its components while they are enjoying the text. Nor is it strictly necessary for writers to carry out such analyses as they write; indeed, the ultimate aim of teaching yourself to write is to make the process of writing as comfortable as the process of reading.

Ideally, writing ought to be like riding a bicycle: something you know how to do without having to think consciously about exactly what it is that you are doing. In order to get to that point, however, it may be necessary to go through a phase when you work step by painful step, planning beginnings and endings, thinking about plot structures, considering alternative viewpoints and learning. Some writers do not need to do this, because it all comes naturally to them, but they are rare – and it certainly does no harm to think more deeply about what the process of writing involves.

Many of the problems which arise in the course of writing fantasy and science fiction stories are common to all kinds of stories. Much of what I say in these pages will, therefore, be applicable to any kind of fiction writing. I shall try to bring the particular problems of writing fantasy and science fiction into clear focus, but in the interests of making this guide as complete as possible I shall not skip over the fundamental aspects of story construction. All I shall take for granted is that would-be writers can spell, punctuate and construct grammatical sentences.

As well as describing the particular problems of writing fantasy and science fiction, and offering practical suggestions as to how they might be solved, I shall attempt to explain why the problems arise and how they affect the various kinds of fantasy and science fiction to be found in the marketplace. The more you understand about the anatomy of stories and the ways in which readers use them the better equipped you will be to find new ways to tackle the perennial problems – and novelty of approach is highly valued in fantasy and science fiction.

I shall not go to great lengths here to describe or define fantasy and science fiction. It is exceedingly difficult to figure out what it is that all stories within any publishing category have, or ought to have, in common – the article on 'Definitions' in the Orbit *Encyclopedia of Science Fiction* consists of six columns of dense and convoluted argument – and if you have picked up this book you probably have as good an idea as anyone else as to what the terms may signify.

From the viewpoint of the writer, the most significant aspect of fantasy and science fiction is that stories of these kinds are either set in imaginary worlds or feature the appearance in the familiar world of some imaginary entity. Although such imaginary intrusions may take different forms in fantasy and science fiction, and may operate according to different rules, the way they function as story devices is very similar. There are far more problems common to both genres than unique to either, so it makes sense to cover them both in the same guidebook.

In subsequent chapters I shall describe the process of constructing real and imaginary worlds and populating them with human and non-human characters in a step-by-step fashion. Before I do that, however, it will be helpful to lay down some general foundations.

The pleasures of creativity

Why should you want to write fantasy and science fiction?

There are, of course, many possible answers to this question and it is highly likely that every writer's motives are mixed. Writers can express ideas and emotions which are important to them but have no other means of expression. Some of these ideas may be fantastic and some of the emotions may be given clearer voice in fantastic fiction. The free exercise of the imagination can be exhilarating, and it offers scope for many kinds of artistry. We are all fantasists at heart; however mundane our everyday lives may be we are all dreamers and daydreamers, and our daydreams are among our most precious and personal possessions.

In the final analysis, what writers love about writing is the power of creativity, and writing fantasy or science fiction offers greater scope for the exercise of that power than writing most other kinds of fiction. With these opportunities – as with all opportunities – come certain difficulties that writers of other kinds of fiction may not have to face, but the reward is worth the risk.

The real world is a vast and complicated place which we must take as we find, but even writers who choose to set their stories in the known world, accepting all its limitations, have a precious kind of power. The power we have to control what happens in our lives is very limited; the richest king there ever was could not control the thoughts and feelings of the most wretched slaves bound to his obedience, but even if you were the poorest writer there ever was, who never sold a line, you would have far greater power over the worlds within your texts than he.

Within your texts nobody, be he slave or king, philosopher or lunatic, can consider a thought or experience a feeling without your say-so. Without your specification, no one within your texts *has* any thoughts or feelings, or any existence at all. Writers of realistic fiction use this power sparingly, but it has no limitations of its own; a writer of fantastic fictions can easily overstep the bounds of actual existence.

Within your texts, *anything* can happen; all you have to do is say so. If the crippled boy requires a miracle before he can walk again, you can work it simply by saying 'and then he got up and walked'. If you want God to descend from his heaven to bow down before the child in question and apologise for putting him in the wheelchair in the first place all you have to do is write it down. Within your story, even God is only one more character (or not, if you care to rule him out); the power of creation rests entirely in *your* hands. Within your story, not a sparrow will fall without your taking the trouble to record it; and if you do not want sparrows to fall, you can save the entire species with a single sentence.

Writing might be unalloyed joy were it not for the fact that power is always shadowed by responsibility. Thankfully, the absolute power that writers have is not weighted down with absolute responsibility. It can be neither suppressed nor diminished, except by choice. All writers know, however, that the joy to be obtained from creativity is not a product of the writing process – actual *writing* is hard work – but a matter of looking back at something written and taking pride in the accomplishment.

Many writers actively hate writing but they love having written, especially if they have written something that seems to them to be worthwhile. This is where the responsibility comes in: if the story is to be reckoned truly worthwhile that judgment has to be endorsed by someone other than the writer. It is good to have godlike power over your creation, but it is even better to have worshipful admirers to inform you that you have exercised that power wisely and well. Because it is done in private and in solitude, it is sometimes possible to forget that writing is essentially an act of communication, but no writer should ever lose sight of the readers.

Writers and readers

It is because writing is addressed to readers that the power of the writer is subject to certain constraints. You, the writer, can do anything at all, but if it is to be worth doing then it must be possible for you, the reader – and, hopefully, for other readers too – to approve of it. Some writers are perfectly content with their own approval, but even they probably feel that such contentment smacks of cowardice. Most writers use their own approval as a kind of filter, to sort out that which should not be crossed-out (or, for those employing advanced technology, not fall prey to the Delete button) before the finished product is submitted for the approval of others.

The absolute power which a writer has to determine what happens within a text can begin to seem rather feeble when the need for reader approval is added to the picture. For this reason, writers exist in rather uneasy relationship to their potential readers, particularly to the editors who function as 'gatekeepers' regulating the flow of texts into the marketplace. The godlike power of the writer can be abruptly reduced to the severely limited power of a humble servant when the completed text falls upon the desk of an editor. Writers fear editors, and sometimes come perilously close to hating them (which helps to explain why so many editors end up married to writers, at least for a while).

Because writers can do anything at all within the worlds of their texts there is a sense in which anyone who can formulate words can be a writer. Because every act of writing assumes a reader, however, there are all kinds of matters which writers have to bear in mind if they are to make what they write intelligible, interesting and admirable. The first and foremost issue which the writer must consider in making this attempt is plausibility. The world within a text must be designed in such a way that it is acceptable to the reader.

It is often assumed that 'plausible' is the same as 'believable', and that 'believable' is the same as 'possible' but in fantasy and science fiction these equivalences break down. If a story is about events which are supposed to have happened in the ordinary course of affairs in the real world then the inclusion of events which the reader considers impossible may indeed make the story unacceptable by rendering it unbelievable. When a story is set in an imaginary world, however, it is much harder to decide and define what is and is not believable *within the context of the story*.

Even a story which begins in the world familiar to the reader may be modified by the intrusion of some magical object, alien being or new invention. Because such intrusions – which I shall call 'novums' – are not ready-made aspects of the familiar world the writer has the freedom to say exactly what they can and cannot do. Even if the novum belongs to a familiar species, it is still adaptable to the writer's whim. For instance, if you want to write a story featuring a vampire you can decide for yourself how much of the conventional image created by Bram Stoker you want to retain, and how much you want to discard. If you want your vampires to be able to operate in daylight all you have to do is say that they can, and if you want to impose conditions limiting their ability to do so you can make up whatever conditions you like.

Any narrative move which turns a story into fantasy is, in essence, one which deliberately crosses the boundary of accepted possibility. A narrative move which turns a story into science fiction is slightly different, in that the 'novum' which it introduces will be represented as something which scientific theory establishes as conceivable but which has not yet been encountered or invented. Introducing such a novum still crosses an important boundary, however, by opening up the question of what might or might not be possible.

Once these kinds of boundaries have been breached, it is no longer sensible to equate plausibility with believability and believability with possibility. Nevertheless, it still makes sense to talk about the plausibility of fantasy and science fiction stories, and about the various features of imaginary worlds to which writers must pay attention if they want their stories to be acceptable to readers. Ideally, of course, we do not want simply to make the worlds within our stories acceptable; we want to make them seductive, or even irresistible – but achieving plausibility is the first step on that road.

Real and imaginary worlds

If it is to be plausible, the world you create within your text needs to be coherent. All its elements should fit together into a satisfactory and appealing whole. You must remember that the world of your story is entirely contained within your text; all the things which the reader needs to know about it have to be written into the text and all the things you write about it ought to be consistent with one another.

Stories which are supposedly set in the real world – including fantasy and science fiction stories in which the real world is supplemented by some kind of 'novum' – have a measure of solidity and internal consistency already built in, 'borrowed' from the world that the writer and reader already know. I shall call these stories 'known-world stories' in order to distinguish them from stories set in imaginary worlds.

Known-world stories have some obvious advantages. If you say that your story is set in London then all the streets and buildings of London – and, for that matter, the rest of the world – will be tacitly present in the world of your story, all neatly laid out and fully functional. Such stories have disadvantages as well; if you borrow your coherency from the real world then you have to be acquainted with all the relevant details of the real world's coherency. If your characters have to take a train from London to Brighton you will need to know the railway station from which trains to Brighton leave and how to get there on the tube. Cashing in on the coherency of the known world requires research.

The burden of accurate reproduction causes many writers to use imaginary settings even when their stories are set in the known world. The characters in various TV soap operas are firmly located within the greater geography of England, Australia or the USA but on a local scale they inhabit streets, or even whole boroughs, which cannot be found on maps. The coherency of fiction is, in fact, dependent on not borrowing *too much* of the coherency of the real world. Giving a detective an address in Baker Street might help him to seem more real, but if he is to be slotted into the reality of Baker Street without actually colliding with the facts the address has to be one that does not actually exist.

Stories which are set in the known world can only take this 'slotting in' process so far. You can set your story in an imaginary town, city, county or state without troubling your readers too much, and you can even slot a small country or two into the Middle East or the heart of Africa, but the bigger your invented space is the greater the pressure it exerts on its borrowed coherency. It used to be easy for writers to insert countries like Ruritania and Graustark into the confused map of middle Europe, but it is far more difficult to do so plausibly now that we are so much better informed.

Inventing towns, cities or countries brings practical problems of its own. You can stock them with whatever buildings you like, arranged to suit the convenience of your plot, but you must spell out those arrangements. Moreover, the things which you invent must be consistent with the realities you have borrowed; they must be the kinds of things that could exist in the midst of real towns, cities or countries.

While your characters were in London intending to go to Brighton you had the advantage that Victoria station was already 'there', whether you had bothered to mention it or not, and your readers can imagine its presence as a 'set' even though you have not described it. On the other hand, when your characters are in Eastleigh intending to go to Buckhampton you are obliged to *invent* the station or bus stop from which they will set out, and this may require a certain amount of descriptive labour if your reader is to be able to picture it as a setting and believe in it as an addendum to the real world.

In fantasy and science fiction stories this kind of narrative labour becomes much more intensive because the settings involved may be much more remote, and the manner in which the imaginary settings 'dovetail' with real settings may be much more complicated. Inventing a plausible alien world may require you to gather many kinds of information – geographical, ecological, historical, technological and so on – into a coherent set. This may require considerable cleverness as well as a good deal of research.

The art of extrapolation

Even if you are working with wholly imaginary worlds, the problem of slotting the imaginary into the real still has to be faced. Stories which are set on planets orbiting distant stars or stories set in a 'secondary world' like Tolkien's Middle-Earth still have to borrow some of their coherency from the reader's acquaintance with the actual world. The worlds in which planetary romances and secondary-world fantasies are set may have an entirely invented geography and an entirely imaginary history but their basic physical conditions are usually transferred without any elaborate commentary from our world. Magic may defy scientific laws but it has to work within the framework of the laws which it violates, as a series of exceptions. Even in the boldest fantasies it is taken for granted that without magic to hold them up, the castles in the clouds would fall, and that without magic to aid her the heroine who is deprived of oxygen will asphyxiate.

Science fiction writers sometimes test the limits of borrowed coherency almost to destruction. Stories have been written about the inhabitants of the surfaces of living worlds or neutron stars, two-dimensional or four-dimensional worlds, and worlds entirely contained within the mind of a dreamer or the software of a computer. The whole point of such exercises is, however, to *extrapolate* coherently from the accepted laws of physics and the known phenomena of chemistry. Even the very rare stories which deliberately alter one of the laws of physics do so in order to examine the logical consequence of making one such change while holding all the other laws constant.

Extrapolation is the key to establishing the coherency of your imaginary worlds. The artistry of fantasy and science fiction stories depends on your ability to figure out what the logical consequences of introducing particular novums may be. This applies just as much to fantasy as to science fiction; magic may be invoked to give your hero three wishes, but you must then figure out how he might choose to use those wishes and what the consequence of each wish would be. The appeal of your story to its readers will depend on your cleverness in figuring out exactly how the wishes are to be fulfilled; such tales usually thrive on the irony of consequences which are wholly logical but unforeseen by the user of the wishes.

You may, if you wish, imagine that there is a contract between yourself and your readers whereby the readers grant you a licence to establish any novum you wish in your story, provided that you promise to look after it properly. Looking after it is exactly what you will have to do; in constructing your story you will be continually asking yourself what would follow, logically, from the situation as it presently stands.

You might think that the simplest and most obvious novums would soon be used up as writers calculated all the likely outcomes of their use, but this is not so. There are any number of ways in which a person granted three wishes might choose to use them, and any number of ways in which their choices might go wrong. The same is true of invisibility, identity exchanges, time machines and all the other staples of playful 'what if?' stories.

When novums are introduced in sets rather than singly – as they have to be in any story of the distant future or any story set in a wholly imaginary world – the possibilities of extrapolation are infinite. Making a future society or an alien world seem coherent can be difficult, because of the hard intellectual labour you have to put into the examination of possible consequences, but it can also be exciting. Some writers become addicted to the business of extrapolation, treating it as a kind of game.

Creating an entire imaginary world can be a lifetime's work, and there are writers who have spent lifetimes doing it. At least some readers felt, as J. R. R. Tolkien did, that they wanted to know a great deal more about Middle-Earth than was revealed in *The Lord of the Rings*, and the supplementary information he assembled now fills a dozen further volumes. It is not unknown for fans of a particular series of stories to become so interested in the world of the story that they long to take part in the extrapolation of its history and imaginary societies; Marion Zimmer Bradley's 'Darkover' series generated the Friends of Darkover, whose members were licensed by the author to set stories of their own there, and it is nowadays common practice for groups of fantasy or science fiction writers to produce 'shared world' story series.

Mercifully, there is a world of difference between coherency and completeness. The exhaustive creative work done by Tolkien in support of Middle-Earth is not compulsory. You do not have to fill in every detail of every world you invent for the purposes of a story; provided that you can maintain the appearance of coherency you can operate on a 'need to know' basis. The artistry of designing plausible imaginary worlds is as much a matter of leaving things out as putting things in; as long as you can convince your reader that everything you actually mention is part of a coherent whole, the whole itself may remain vague.

The minimum that your reader needs to know is everything that is essential to the workings of your plot, plus as much additional information as may be required to bind that information into a satisfactory set. You need to reassure your reader that the various elements of your imaginary world do fit together – that the world *makes sense* –

but that can usually be achieved simply by making sure that there are no glaring inconsistencies.

The longer your story is, the more detail you will need to fill in if you are to maintain the illusion that the world of the story really is a plausible world, and the more work you will have to do to make sure that the details do fit together in a logical fashion. In many short stories, however, it is only necessary to provide a 'slice of life' which does not have to get to grips with ponderous matters of history, ecology and so on. As long as you can include a few significant details that are cleverly linked together you will do enough to captivate your readers.

Plausibility and probability

Readers who object to the use of anything explicitly supernatural in stories often overlook the fact that supposedly realistic plots are often so wildly improbable as to be absurd. We are all used to seeing characters in stories defy the calculus of probability with casual ease. We know perfectly well when we get to the end of a story that if the heroine is hanging from a window-ledge by her fingertips it will not even matter if she lets go; the hero will still contrive to grab her and haul her to safety. Whenever the hero of a story says that 'it's a million-to-one chance but it just might work' the move is virtually certain to succeed. In stories – especially in the climaxes of stories – heroes can always do what needs to be done, no matter how unlikely it seems.

There is, in fact, no 'probability' at all within the world of a text. There are no matters of chance and no coincidences. A character in a story may throw a pair of dice or draw a card from a pack, but the outcome of any such action is decided by the writer. If the writer decides that the character will throw double six or draw the ace of spades that is what will happen. It is, of course, open to you to throw dice or draw a card in order to determine what you will write next, but that is a calculated abdication of choice, not a matter of chance – and the likelihood is that the story produced by the dice or the cards will be lousy. The 999,999 cases in which the million-to-one shot didn't work remained unrecorded because they had no value as stories.

This observation puts the quest for plausibility into a slightly different light. Your readers are *participants* in your story and they have an active interest in its construction and continuity. They want the story to make sense and to form a satisfactory whole, and will welcome anything you do towards that end. They also want the story to be exciting, and will be sympathetic to any device you use to enhance its excitement. Because readers like stories to keep moving, and eventually to arrive somewhere interesting, you have a licence to engineer all kinds of opportunities and coincidences without regard to matters of probability. In the worlds within texts every decaying rope-bridge is certain to hold together just long enough – or, if it breaks, will allow the hero to clamber up the limp remnant to safety – and every honeymooning couple whose car breaks down at night is sure to find that the one lighted window they can see in the distance belongs to a haunted house. The unlikelihood of such occurrences is no threat to plausibility.

The readers' willingness to accept improbabilities which serve to keep the plot moving is more than matched by their willingness to accept improbabilities that make a contribution to the integrity of the story, binding its parts into a whole. For instance, literary dreams usually serve this sort of purpose.

If real dreams serve any purpose at all we have no idea what it is. In spite of our tendency to search them for insights and omens, their meanings remain stubbornly unclear and they remain obstinately devoid of any prophetic power. Literary dreams, on the other hand, are *always* meaningful and sometimes uncannily prophetic; if they were not they would have no place in the story at all. Literary dreams must be revelatory, at least so far as the reader is concerned, and most readers are only too happy to overlook the fact that real dreams are not like that. Even in known-world fiction, dreams invariably serve this kind of integrative function, but in fantasy and science fiction dreamlike visions can be granted much greater powers, and routinely are.

The most elaborate attempt to account for the meaning of real dreams was, of course, advanced by Sigmund Freud, who attempted to read them as symbolic accounts of his patients' anxieties and neuroses. Whether this kind of analysis has any use in clinical practice is unclear, but its utility in constructing and decoding literary dreams is considerable. Nor is it only dreams that can be symbolic in stories; the predicaments of the characters can be mirrored in all kinds of ways: by the weather, by the presence and fate of significant objects, by the blooming and fading of flowers, by the strange behaviour of animals, and so on. In a story, everything observed and everything that transpires may have a meaning within the story's scheme that objects and events rarely, if ever, have in the real world.

When readers detect the symbolism of objects or events within a plot, or perceive patterns made by the recurrence of particular motifs or events that echo earlier events, they are not offended by the improbability of such contrivances. Readers *like* to discover such links and unities, and their pleasing qualities are more likely to add to the plausibility of the tale than detract from it. All these devices are available to you for use in securing the coherency of your stories, in addition to the logic of extrapolation.

The moral order of worlds within texts

The fact that readers are so very willing to entertain improbabilities in the stories they read informs us that the most important aspect of the coherency of imaginary worlds is not a matter of logical consistency. The main reason is that those improbabilities usually work, at least in the end, to the advantage of the heroes and the disadvantage of the villains.

The real world does not distribute its rewards and punishments according to any discernible moral order. As Saint Matthew and everyone else has observed, the rain falls on the just and the unjust alike. The wicked are no more likely than the good to be struck by lightning or devoured by cancer, and the virtuousness of the good offers no perceptible protection from suffering and misfortune. Many people insist that there must be a further life after death where the moral account books will be balanced and we will all get what we really deserve, but not everyone can believe that – and in the meantime, we must seek what solace we can in stories where things work out differently.

As the writer of a story, you always have the power to make things come out right: to make the guilty suffer and to reward the innocent. You may have good reasons for not wanting to do that, and your reader may sympathise with those reasons, but you do need to bear in mind that the decisions you make in constructing your plot have this kind of 'moral weight'. In much the same way that the world of your story requires a certain logical coherency, the events that occur there require a certain moral coherency. This does not mean that you must always operate as a benevolent creator, but it does mean that you must bear the responsibility of the benevolence you refuse.

It is because of their relationship to moral order that the events in stories *matter* so much to their readers. We are joyful when the heroine of a story achieves her heart's desire because we feel that she *deserves* it – and we feel this so strongly that we experience a sharp sensation of sorrow if, instead, the unfolding logic of events within the story brings her to despair or destruction. Your power to move your readers – to make them happy or sad – is based in their willingness to care about your characters, and that willingness is rooted in their desire to see justice done. However remote the world of your story is from the known world in terms of its physics or geography, and no matter what kinds of magic or superscience operate there, it is as tightly bound to our notions of moral order as the most accurate reflection of the known world.

Our capacity to 'identify' with characters in fiction is not at all dependent on similarity. Anyone who has been part of an audience watching Steven Spielberg's film *E.T.* or J. M. Barrie's play *Peter Pan* must have seen large numbers of people reduced to tears by the plight of imaginary characters who resemble us not at all – so little, in fact, that the part of E.T. is played by a plastic doll and the part of Tinkerbell by a spotlight.

The reason that we have such considerable sympathy for these non-human characters, while we righteously loathe the all-too-human foes who threaten them, is purely a matter of moral compatibility. The simple fact is that we love the good guys, whoever and whatever they may be, and we hate the bad guys. When E.T. finally goes home and Tinkerbell is applauded back to life after drinking the poison which Captain Hook intended for Peter we feel uplifted – so uplifted that we may weep with joy in a way we very rarely have occasion to do in response to real events.

We feel uplifted, too, whenever the villain in a story goes bloodily to his destruction, although in these instances we are more likely to cheer than weep. We do not cheer because we are sadists who revel in the pain and ignominy of others but because we recognise the moral propriety of the villain's consignment to a hellish end. (Unfortunately, this fact is overlooked in most discussions about the role and effects of violence in the media, which is why so many of those discussions are futile.)

Once we have recognised this, we can easily understand why most people would rather read stories with happy endings than stories in which the pressure of 'realism' causes writers to withhold rewards for the good or to let the wicked get away scot-free. We can also understand why it is that so many readers like to read the same kind of book repeatedly. What these readers are doing is participating in a ritual of moral affirmation whose force depends on continual repetition – in which respect it is similar to all the other kinds of affirmative rituals with which we are familiar: legal rituals, religious rituals and the rituals of petty superstition.

The importance of these observations to you, as a writer of fantasy and science fiction, is that the imaginary beings that you create can always command the intense interest of readers, provided that you can make the readers care what happens to them. You can achieve that by placing them in difficulties and dilemmas which bring the readers' moral assumptions into play. Indeed, imaginary beings operating in wholly fantastic worlds may display moral issues in a 'purer' way than any real-world situation could. This is why talking animals are so often used to dramatise moral advice, why the plots of fantasy novels often take the form of all-out battles between Good and Evil, and why moralistic fantasies play such an important role in fiction written for children.

It is not, of course, *necessary* for you to frame your stories as fables with tacit or explicit morals – but you will find that many of the stories you write do have the quality of a fable, even if you do not consciously plan them that way. The willingness of your readers to pity characters who are unjustly persecuted, no matter what kind of creatures they are, and to identify with the hopeful ambitions of the downtrodden, is the greatest advantage you have as a writer. It will licence all kinds of improbable inventions and may well compensate for any small errors or inadequacies that afflict your logical extrapolations.

Tragedy and comedy

The fact that most readers prefer endings in which good triumphs and evil are confounded does not mean that writers are obliged to provide them – although writers working in certain sectors of the marketplace may find that they are under very heavy pressure to do so. Although your readers may be grateful to you for providing a morally uplifting ending you do have other options which preserve other kinds of coherency.

One option you have is to use your refusal to make things work out happily to generate the special feeling of sorrow and frustration which we call *tragedy*. If you end your story with a sober and calculatedly harrowing violation of moral order, your readers will know that they are being instructed to recognise and lament the fact that, in real life, misfortune often falls upon the good and wickedness often goes unpunished.

Nowadays, of course, we apply the word 'tragedy' to all kinds of events in the real world but its original meaning pertained strictly to works of art. This broadening of application reflects the habit which newswriters have of turning events into stories in order to make them more interesting and more engaging. When we are asked to think of a real event as a tragedy we are being asked to consider it as a refusal of moral order rather than an absence of it.

The feeling of tragedy is, however, not the only one associated with episodes in stories in which characters are frustrated in their aims. There are other effects at which you might aim, the most obvious alternative being comedy. Although its emotional effect is nearly opposite, the essence of comedy is closer than you might think to the essence of tragedy. Laughter and weeping are so closely allied that one may lead to the other, and we are all familiar with such observations as 'you have to laugh, or else you'd cry'. It is not only 'black comedy' that has a hint of cruelty about it; 'slapstick' generally features blows and pratfalls that would be very painful were they not fictitious.

If you can make the failures of your characters sufficiently absurd, or even sufficiently prolific, your readers will know that they are being invited to laugh rather than cry. Most comedies are, in effect, little more than extended chronicles of failure and frustration in which the hapless heroes are battered and bruised by the vicissitudes of fate but always bounce back. In many such accounts – examples abound in animated cartoons, *The Hitch-Hiker's Guide to the Galaxy* and Terry Pratchett's Discworld novels (whose most popular character is Death) – large-scale disasters and extraordinary acts of violence and cruelty are routinely made to seem funny, often deliberately emphasising the thinness of the line that separates tragedy from comedy.

Many comedies confine the humiliations to which they subject their characters to the mid-sections of their stories, ultimately resolving their plots with conventional happy endings, but many are content to end with one pratfall even more spectacular than all the rest. These variations serve to remind us that stories may serve several different functions, of which the ritual is merely the most common. Pain may be nasty but it is vital to our well-being because it offers us warnings when we are in grave danger; were we incapable of feeling pain reck-lessness would lead us quickly to destruction. We do need the feeling of uplift that is delivered by stories with happy endings, but we must also learn to cope with the fact that the stories we are constantly trying to discover or create in our real lives will continually run into difficulties.

For this reason, while writers who always write stories with happy endings may earn the undying affection of their readers, writers who can turn their hand to tragedy may also earn undying respect. Comedians can go either way; those who cultivate respect rather than affection are usually known as satirists. All these options are open to you, but it is worth bearing in mind that the legendary last words of the famous actor – 'Dying is easy; comedy is hard' – apply only to stagecraft. For writers, tragedy and comedy are both difficult to contrive by comparison with conventional happy endings.

2
ONCE UPON A TIME: BEGINNINGS

What is to be done?

In Rudyard Kipling's *Just So Stories*, immediately after the tale of 'The Elephant's Child', there is a poem which begins:

> I keep six honest serving-men
> (They taught me all I knew);
> Their names are What and Why and When
> And How and Where and Who.

These are the six questions you have to bear in mind when beginning to write a story. Not every story requires you to establish all six, and some may require you not to do so. Some stories require you to keep one vital item of information up your sleeve so that you can reveal it with a sudden flourish at the appropriate time. Even so, you must establish everything that the reader needs to know in order to get a grip on the story.

In a short story you must do this work as swiftly and as neatly as possible. Novels have much more scope for characters and settings to be introduced at a leisurely pace, so that the groundwork may be tackled in a relatively unhurried fashion – which often involves several distinct 'beginnings', each introducing a different setting and cast of characters – but even in a novel it makes sense to tackle the six points methodically.

This kind of groundwork has to be done in any kind of story, but writing fantasy and science fiction requires you to grapple with additional problems, because the answers to the six questions may be much more exotic. This gives you additional scope for tantalising your readers with mysteries, but it also adds to the danger that if you do not do your introductory work efficiently and thoroughly you may leave your reader hopelessly confused.

It is not difficult, when writing about the real world, to specify where and when a story is taking place. A single place-name and a date will usually do the job adequately, although readers will need to be provided with the relevant details of places and times with which they are not very familiar. In known-world stories it is sometimes not necessary to specify the time at all, because readers tend to begin stories with the provisional assumption that they are set in the present, and they will usually continue to assume that unless and until the text lets them know otherwise. In much the same way, readers of known-world stories can readily pick up hints and cues which allow them to figure out what is going on and how the characters are tackling their problems without the writer having to provide elaborate explanations. Fantasy and science fiction stories are problematic, not merely because so much more needs to be spelled out, but also because readers might take entirely the wrong inference from ill-judged or unintended hints and cues.

Fantasy and science fiction stories can be set anywhere or in any time, including countless places which have no possible location within any map and times which cannot possibly be linked to the episodes of actual history. The events which are taking place there may be bizarre, and the characters may be able to do things that ordinary humans cannot. This means that you might have to provide elaborate explanations before your readers are able to orientate themselves within the world of your story – but you must do so in such a way that your story still captures the readers' attention and engages their interest. If readers have to plough through a prefatory essay before the story itself gets started, some of them may decide not to bother.

The tactics of introduction

It is often a good idea to let your readers know immediately that your story is not set in the familiar world by inserting a 'distancing move' into the first sentence, as George Orwell does with the reference to the clocks striking thirteen in the opening sentence of *Nineteen Eighty-four*. The main function of such a ploy is to make your readers wary, so that they will not take too much for granted as they read your opening paragraphs. Orwell's observation serves to warn his readers that the odour of boiled cabbage and the rag mats which Winston Smith encounters at the beginning of the next paragraph might not carry the same implications that they would in a known-world story, and makes the poster whose caption reads 'Big Brother is watching you' more sinister than it would be if the reader were still assuming (in spite of the title) that the story is set in the present day.

Some kinds of fantasy story have been around so long that their tellers have developed brief formulas to alert their hearers or readers to the type of story with which they were dealing. The most famous of these is 'Once upon a time', which signals to a reader that the story is likely to be set in a distant but unspecified past and is likely to feature fairies, witches, magic and animals that talk alongside – or even instead of – human characters.

The 'all-purpose fantasy-land' conjured up by the 'Once upon a time' formula expanded over time as the tellers of folktales exported and imported materials over larger and larger distances, functioning as a melting-pot for the myths and legends of many particular cultures. Modern fantasy has, however, become so very diverse that such simple formulas are no longer very helpful and they are rarely employed today without a hint of humorous condescension.

It is less than a hundred years since the problem of how to begin a science fiction story was very awkward indeed. Every author had then to accept that the very notion of setting a story in the future or in another world would be unfamiliar to the reader and rather startling. In all the pioneering science fiction that H. G. Wells wrote there is not a single story that actually *begins* in the future or in an alien environment. Usually, Wells's characters are introduced with ponderous prefaces firmly anchored in the here-and-now before being displaced by careful and studied narrative moves into the future (in *The Time Machine*), another dimension (in 'The Plattner Story') or another world (in *The First Men in the Moon*). Although Wells's novella 'A Story of the Days to Come' is set in 2100 he felt obliged to equip his story with a baldly descriptive title, to introduce it with an essay which painstakingly compares everyday life in his own world with everyday life as it might be lived in the year it was written, and to make the characters refer continually to the present day for the sake of comparison and contrast.

Science fiction was always too diverse to make much use of a formula like 'Once upon a time' but the invention of the genre label and the development of science fiction magazines made things much easier for writers. The readers who bought science fiction magazines knew better than to begin a story with the assumption that it would be set here and now; on the contrary, they began with the expectation that it would probably be set in the future and quite possibly on an alien world. Editors of such magazines were usually able to provide extra hints in the form of brief blurbs, and writers who knew that they would get that kind of help could take the view that the burden of explanation need not weigh so heavily upon their opening paragraphs. Even if you can take such support for granted, however – and there are still many places of publication which cannot provide it – the problem of welcoming your readers to the world of your story is still something that requires careful attention.

If too much introductory information is delivered with brutal directness it is bound to seem very awkward. Beginning a story set in the year 2100 with a brief sketch of all the changes which have overtaken the world in the last hundred years is never seductive, however vital the listed facts might be to the reader's understanding of your story. Lumps of 'raw information' may be less off-putting if they are inserted into your narrative after it has built up momentum, but even then it may be politic to keep them reasonably small and as unobtrusive as possible. The problem of how to *introduce* your future to the reader still remains.

So important is this problem to science fiction writers that they have developed a special jargon for its discussion, in which packages of pure information are called 'info-dumps' and the process of getting information across is called 'info-dumping'. Opinions vary as to which strategies of info-dumping are the most useful and the most artful, but it is universally accepted that beginning a story with a solid info-dump is a very bad idea. If you are to capture the attention and goodwill of your readers you need to leak information into your text as unobtrusively as possible, or at least to 'decorate' the information in such a way as to make it more interesting. Anything which is not immediately vital to the story's comprehension may be best left for later disclosure.

Today, you can assume that every reader has some awareness of the possibility that a story might be set in an imaginary environment, but readers still differ a great deal in the extent to which they can use that awareness. Habitual readers of specialist magazines tend to develop skills which allow them to orientate themselves very quickly, and find stories which do too much preparatory work slow and clumsy. On the other hand, some readers will say that they simply 'cannot read' science fiction – and what they usually mean by that is that they do not have the skills required to get to grips with science fiction stories whose openings are designed for an informed audience. For this reason, there is no simple answer to the question of how much introductory work you need to do, or what the best way is to do it.

When?

The time of a story can usually be established simply by mentioning a date. Unfortunately, the date will not mean much without some supporting information. If the story is set in the future you will need to provide some information about what has happened between the present day and the date of the story. If the story is set in the past your readers will probably need some help to remind them what kinds of things were happening around that time.

There are some kinds of science fiction story in which questions of 'when' become confused. In 'alternative history' stories which deal with events which might have unfolded had some incident in history turned out differently, the date of the story is important precisely because it will be associated with events other than those which took place in the known world. If such a story is set in 'the present day', the present in question need not be *our* present and the reader will need to be made aware of that. The ways in which the present of the story differ from our present will need to be made clear, and you will have to think carefully about the sequence of hints that you intend to drop and the manner in which you intend to lay them out.

For example, my alternative history novel *The Empire of Fear* begins with a paragraph which combines the function of offering basic information about the time of the story with a distancing move which is supposed to alert readers to the fact that it is an alternative history: 'It was the thirteenth of June in the year of Our Lord 1623. Warm weather had come early to Grand Normandy and the streets of London were bathed in sunlight.' The fourth paragraph of the story refers to 'Prince Richard', further emphasising the fact that *this* 1623 is not our 1623 – a point further underlined when it is revealed that the Richard in question is Richard the Lionheart, now approaching his 466th birthday (by virtue of having become a vampire of sorts). The intermediate paragraphs establish that the world of the story is otherwise much the same as the seventeenth century with which we are familiar.

As *The Empire of Fear* continues to unwind it continually juxtaposes items of fact common to both histories with ones which belong solely to the imaginary history of the alternative world. The event which set the history of this alternative Europe on its distinctive path is revealed on page 16, where it is noted that the vampiric Attila the Hun conquered Rome, although the root cause of the alteration which allowed Attila to become a vampire is not clearly identified until a much later point in the story. In spite of all my best efforts, however, I did get one very irate letter from a reader who had set the book aside in disgust on discovering that Richard the Lionheart was occupying the throne of 'Grand Normandy' in 1623, assuming that this was appalling ignorance rather than ingenious design.

There are, of course, other kinds of story in which questions of 'when' are not connected with the when of the present day at all. A secondary world may well have a history which runs parallel to ours and occasionally intersects with it (as the history of C. S. Lewis's Narnia does) but it may well be entirely disconnected from 'real' time. Even if the timing of a story is only significant with respect to other events in the world of the story, some sense of temporal sequence has to be communicated to the reader. For instance, Chapter 1 of *The Lord of the Rings* begins by establishing that sixty years have passed since the events recorded in *The Hobbit*, and twelve since Bilbo's adoption of Frodo, although the 'true' time-scale of the story, extending from the forging of the ring of power to the aftermath of its destruction, is introduced more gradually.

Time in the worlds within fantasy texts may also be connected to our time in a calculatedly perverse way, as in the many tales of Faerie in which mortals who stray into the parallel world for a few hours or days find that years have elapsed when they return home. Here, as in many science fiction stories involving time travel, the dislocation of time is the central theme of the story and if you intend to write a story of this sort you may have to pay special attention to the cultivation of a sense of time. Generally speaking, if time is the subject matter of your story it makes sense to multiply the number of references – both explicit and subtle – that you make to it.

Where?

Even when you are dealing with imaginary locations a great deal can be accomplished with a name, and it is usually a good idea to include such a name in the first paragraph. The mere mention of the United States of Europe, Mars, Alpha Centauri, Atlantis, Hyperborea or Camelot will serve to let your readers know whereabouts they are (and what kind of story they are likely to be dealing with).

Even names that you make up may carry all kinds of implications. Eastleigh is obviously an English rural village, probably of the quaint variety, while any name ending in '-chester' is likely to suggest a larger town. Towns and associated geographical features in the United States of America can be neatly 'characterised' by names recognisably borrowed from an Ameriindian language, while places in Australia and New Zealand can be set in context with terms borrowed from Aboriginal and Maori languages. The more bizarre a name is the more firmly it is distanced from the here and now – and the better it will serve in consequence as a distancing device. For instance, one does not have to be familiar with the works of Clark Ashton Smith to figure out that Averoigne is likely to be closer to home than Zothique, or that a story set in Sfanomoë or Uzuldaroum is likely to be as exotic in subject matter as it is in nomenclature.

As with dates, place-names are rarely adequate in themselves to create a sense of place; they will certainly need further support and may need it quickly. You must also bear in mind that the implications already built into place-names can be treacherous as well as helpful. Ray Bradbury's Mars is not the same place as Kim Stanley Robinson's Mars and T. H. White's Camelot is not the same place as Mary Stewart's Camelot, so you must be careful to make sure that if you refer to Mars or Camelot you provide adequate supplementary information as soon as possible.

It is possible to establish the where of your story by describing the first scene from an objective point of view, paying appropriate attention to matters of geographical detail, the nature of any nearby buildings and other large-scale artifacts, and so on. You must, however, be careful that such descriptions do not build up into unwieldy info-dumps.

A sense of place can usually be cultivated more deftly and more delicately by leaving the job of description to your viewpoint character, telling the reader what she sees as she looks about her. This method is relatively easy to spin out, leaking information by degrees into an account of what the character is doing and saying. It also has the advantage of allowing you to make the character pay special attention to significant and revealing details, perhaps by noticing something of particular interest or something out of the ordinary. Whenever a character notices something out of the ordinary it usually serves a dual function: it calls attention to the detail itself while indirectly conveying information about the 'normality' it is defying.

There are some kinds of stories in which 'where' is deliberately left unspecified in the introduction, so that it may remain a mystery, at least for a while. A common type of story produced by inexperienced writers is one in which the vaguely specified characters are moving through what appears to be a bizarre alien landscape which will be revealed in the last line of the story to be something familiar seen from an odd angle. For instance, characters marching through the brown tangled undergrowth of a vast forest of huge plastic spires might ultimately be revealed to be microbes on a hairbrush. Stories of this kind are sometimes called 'concealed-environment' stories, although that term seems far too polite to editors who see dozens of them and can come to loathe them intensely.

Writers who think this kind of narrative move is a clever idea tend to overestimate the willingness of readers to be delighted by their cleverness and you would probably be wise to steer clear. Such stories are of some technical interest, however, in that they overturn the usual problems involved in beginning a story; instead of having to specify where the story is taking place the writer must take all kinds of precautions to avoid the where of the story becoming obvious too soon. This can easily lead to absurd circumlocutions, whereby the writer is forced to extraordinary lengths to avoid calling a spade a spade (or, in the hairbrush example, a bristle a bristle).

Concealed-environment stories of a more interesting kind form a small subgenre of science fiction. Stories of this kind often involve travellers on a 'generation starship' who have forgotten that they are in transit and have come to think of the ship as the entire universe; examples include Robert A. Heinlein's 'Universe' and Brian Aldiss's *Non-Stop* (which an American editor with no sense at all of the propriety of such tales once retitled *Starship*). In this kind of story the question of where the characters might be becomes an element of mystery with sufficient force to drive the plot along. The task of describing the environment in such a way as to create a sense of place without actually giving the game away may become very challenging. As in any mystery story the readers must be given enough information to ensure that the ultimate revelation will fit all the recorded data, but not so much that they will guess, long before the characters do, exactly what the true situation is.

If you intend to write a story of this kind you should contrive to slip a vital detail into an early paragraph whose significance will become suddenly and strikingly clear at a much later point in the story. If you are clever, you may be able to insert a whole series of such teasing details into your story at measured intervals.

Who?

As with places, much can be said about characters simply by naming them, and it is usually a good idea to name them immediately. Inexperienced writers often begin stories with the actions and thoughts of a character who is identified as 'he' or 'the woman' but this can become very confusing as soon as they start interacting with other characters, especially if these are introduced as 'her daughter' or 'the second man'. Because *you* always know who your characters are and what each of them is doing it is easy to leave your reader with insufficient information about such matters.

If in doubt, it is always safest to spell out as quickly as possible exactly who is doing what, and exactly how they are related to one another. A further dimension of complexity may be added to the problem of introducing your characters if one of them is to address the reader directly, in first-person narrative. Again, because you know who the 'I' of your story is, it is easy to forget that your readers need to be told who she is. The days when first-person narrators routinely began their accounts by formally introducing themselves are gone, so you may need to find other ways of subtly letting drop the narrator's name, sex and occupation. Readers can become disorientated if they suddenly find out halfway through the story that a narrator they had assumed to be male is actually female.

In fantasy and science fiction stories the business of introducing characters is further complicated by the fact that characters may not be human. As well as specifying the category that such characters belong to – elves, robots, giants, aliens, and so on – you may also have to specify exactly what kind of elves or aliens are to be featured in *this* story and exactly what marks this *particular* elf or alien apart from his fellows.

It is as well to bear in mind when starting a story that once you have established in the readers' minds that the tale is fantastic you have established a context of expectation in which *any* character might, in principle, be unhuman. This means that if you are vague about the species to which particular characters belong your readers might jump to an odd conclusion or think there is a mystery where you did not intend to establish one. You may have to take great care to make sure that your readers know as much as they need to know about what kinds of being the characters in your story are.

Some writers make it a policy not to say very much about their leading characters – especially if they are using a first-person narrator – in case it interferes with the reader's identification with the character. Writers of this kind may deliberately refrain from offering elaborate physical descriptions of key characters and offer their protagonist to readers as a kind of 'blank space' into whose shoes any and all readers may easily step. If it is necessary to the story that the protagonist works in a bank or plays football they will establish that fact and that fact alone. Other writers, by contrast, may assume that the story will not really 'come alive' for the reader unless the reader can be given a fairly detailed account of what sort of individual the protagonist of the story is and what the other major characters are like. Writers of this kind will normally try to assist the reader's imagination by giving various hints that help the reader to picture the characters and items of information which fill out their personal histories, even if these are irrelevant to the story. Neither one of these strategies is ideal; different readers have different preferences.

If the work of establishing the characters in the story is done simply by listing points of appearance and biographical details the lists can easily build into awkward info-dumps. As with places, it helps to locate visual descriptions within the reported impressions of a viewpoint character, who can not only call attention to significant features but can also make useful comparisons. Modern writers frequently provide visual cues by having the viewpoint character liken other characters to well-known actors – or even to particular roles in well-known films or TV shows – but there is less scope for this kind of ploy in fantasy and science fiction than in thrillers or romances. Comparing the appearance of a character in a story set in the twenty-second century to Robert Redford is bound to seem anachronistic.

The problems of introducing information about what your characters look like and what kinds of work they do are not trivial – especially if the world of your story has a range of occupations very different from the everyday world – but they are less vexatious than the problem of revealing what *kind* of person each character is: brave or cowardly, intelligent or stupid, dreamy or down-to-earth. Strategies of characterisation will be discussed in much greater detail in chapter 5, but if it is crucial to your story that the character is a coward or a dreamer that fact must be established as close to the beginning of the story as you can contrive and you must do more than simply *say so*. You must establish the vital attribute by offering a revealing example. If you are introducing the character at second-hand you can do this brutally, by having your narrator say 'Dave was the kind of guy who...' but you still need to think up an impulsive act or a response to awkward circumstance that will sum up the character and show him for what he is. When establishing 'who', demonstration is always more effective than explanation.

As well as 'concealed-environment' stories, there are 'concealed-identity' stories, in which the identity of the narrator is carefully kept secret until the final revelation. Inexperienced writers are especially fond of writing stories in which the narrator eventually turns out to be a dog or a cat. Inexperienced science fiction writers are astonishingly fond of writing stories in which the survivors of a cosmic disaster turn out to be called Adam and Eve. This latter move and related variants – including those in which the mysterious narrator turns out to be God or the Devil – have been lumped together by Brian Aldiss as 'Shaggy God stories'. Stories in which the 'characters' turn out be icons in a computer game are nearly as common, and just as tedious.

Although trivial concealed-identity stories do get into print occasionally it is as well to remember that editors see an awful lot of them; the editor of a 1970s' science fiction magazine once told me that one in every three submissions she received was a story of this kind. As with concealed-environment stories, however, there is a more sophisticated variety which forms a virtual sub-genre of fantasy and science fiction: the 'amnesiac' story in which the protagonist either does not know or is mistaken about who (or what) he is.

The reason why this kind of story often works very well in fantasy and science fiction is that the range of possible answers to the question 'who' is much wider than that available in naturalistic fiction. There are also many more plausible devices that may be invoked to explain the character's ignorance or delusion. A story whose opening paragraphs introduce a character whose identity is a mystery can make productive use of the force of the protagonist's desire to find out who she really is in capturing and holding the reader's interest.

What?

The 'what' of a story is usually an event, although in fantasy and science fiction stories it is often an unusual entity.

You may find it useful to get your stories off to a flying start by pitching the reader straight into a dramatic situation or a combative argument, perhaps opening with the hero taking evasive action or with a dramatic line of dialogue. This is very often done in short stories, which must hurry along lest they become overlong, but novels sometimes begin with a short dramatic 'teaser' which attempts to get the reader hooked before reverting to a more painstaking and measured series of introductions to the principal characters and settings.

Normally, the event which begins a story – or the entity which is the story's focal point – establishes a challenge to which the characters must respond, thus launching a plot with sufficient momentum to get it moving at the right pace. I shall leave more elaborate discussion of challenges and responses until the next chapter, but the event in question is usually either an unfortunate disruption of the characters' routine or a welcome opportunity which they are avid to seize. In fantasy and science fiction stories the challenges with which characters are faced may be very exotic indeed. This allows tremendous scope for originality, but it also puts a considerable burden on the ingenuity of the writer.

Writers who focus on real problems which characters may face in the real world have a considerable legacy of real experience to draw upon. For instance, anyone who wants to write a story about a kidnapping can go to a library and consult books which describe and analyse the experiences of actual kidnap victims, using that as a resource to make their own story ring true. If you want to write a story about a world in which there are three sexes instead of two, however, you will have no factual sources to refer to. Apart from your own powers of extrapolation the only authorities you can consult for guidance will be other stories with similar themes.

The challenges which are featured in fantasy or science fiction stories usually involve strange events and alien entities. Indeed, the events are often so strange as to seem inexplicable and the entities are often so alien as to be deeply enigmatic. Most such stories ultimately allow the seemingly inexplicable to be explained and the enigmas to be unravelled but there is a substantial subset in which the whole point of the story is that no explanation is possible and no understanding achievable.

In most fantasy and science fiction stories the 'what' of the story is what I have called its novum (other commentators prefer the term 'motif' and many think that 'idea' is perfectly adequate). It may, of course, be an exotic character rather than a thing or an event – in fantasy and science fiction the question 'who?' sometimes becomes 'who or what?'

Although many novums – time machines, wishing rings, antigravity devices, cloaks of invisibility and so on – are used repeatedly, and may need only to be named, most will need fairly careful specification. This will often require a substantial info-dump, which is best left until your story has built up momentum, but the beginning of your story must at least pave the way for a more exhaustive description. If you are working with a genuinely new novum the opening paragraphs of your story may have to lay down a good deal of groundwork to allow your readers to get a firm grip on its nature.

This kind of introductory groundwork is often best laid down in dialogue. If your central character has to stumble across an unfamiliar object or take part in some exotic ritual it is always convenient to have someone with whom she can discuss the matter, so that its problematic aspects can be highlighted.

In many fantasy and science fiction stories the 'what?' of the story is derived from a 'what if?' and the extrapolation of a fanciful notion becomes the driving force of its plot. This type of story is sometimes called an 'idea as hero' story because the characters and settings in the story are selected or designed in such a way as to display the idea to its best advantage. More will be said about constructing this type of story in the next chapter but it needs to be noted here that considerable thought may be required as to how best to introduce such an idea so that the extrapolation of its possibilities can be organised neatly and effectively.

Many stories whose novums are to be patiently extrapolated or introduced by degrees into the everyday world try to develop a 'crescendo' effect by starting with a small and enigmatic disruption of the patterns of everyday life and proceeding through increasingly assertive revelations to a climactic confrontation. For instance, M. R. James used a method of ghost-story construction in which the first manifestation of his supernatural visitors was merely curious, the second sinister and the third outrightly shocking. Beginning such a story usually involves establishing the familiarity of the background while carefully adding a tiny jarring detail. Many stories extrapolating the potential of a new invention begin with modest applications and continue to add more and more until the whole society is transformed; Bob Shaw's 'slow glass' stories combined in the episodic novel *Other Days, Other Eyes* offer a fine example of such a crescendo of social change.

By contrast, many stories – especially ones which are set in far futures or in exotic secondary Worlds – start with a flourish by placing some key aspect of the imaginary world in the foreground of the very first scene, using it as a stridently melodramatic distancing device. One of the delights of writing fantasy and science fiction is that you can often put a 'punch-line' at the beginning of a story as well as the end. For instance, Henry Kuttner's novel *The Far Reality* opens with the line 'The doorknob opened a blue eye and looked at him.'

Why?

The 'why' of a story arises out of the interaction of the 'who' and the 'what', and as such is closely related to the 'how'. Most 'why' questions are to do with the motivation of the characters. Why is the heroine so interested in the object she has found? Why is the event which begins the story such a terrible threat to the hero?

It helps to make a story work if you pay close attention to the early establishment of the motives that will propel your characters through your story. In particular, it helps when planning or beginning a story to set things up in such a way that the situation you intend to sketch out will be *especially* alluring or problematic for the central character, who will thus be given a powerful reason for wanting to get to grips with it – or to get out of it with the least possible delay.

It helps enormously to create tension and build up narrative drive if your central character finds the phenomenon which confronts him as the story begins, or the event in which he is immediately caught up, more puzzling or more threatening than any other person would. The customary advice given to writers in search of a way to build a particular novum into a plot is to ask themselves: 'Who will get hurt?' If you want your story to grip the reader it makes sense to ensure that the central character is driven by the most powerful and urgent motives you can contrive.

The question of who will get hurt is particularly relevant to fantasy and science fiction stories of the 'idea as hero' kind. If you want to write a story about an exotic society it is often convenient to describe it from the point of view of a misfit or rebel who feels the full weight of its oddities and injustices. If you want to write a story about the transforming power of a new invention it is often convenient to look at it from the point of view of someone who will be thrown out of work by it, or someone who will not be able to reap the benefits it offers to others.

In many fantasy and science fiction mystery stories the 'why' question which occupies centre stage is not the why of the protagonist's motives but the why of someone else's motives. The exotic characters which may populate fantasy and science fiction stories frequently exhibit strange behaviour which more ordinary characters must strive to understand. Thus, for instance, Isaac Asimov was able to devise a whole series of robot stories in which an expert robopsychologist had to figure out why the three laws of robotics were causing robots to behave in apparently nonsensical ways.

Although answers to 'why' questions which are left carefully unanswered until a climactic revelation can be as bathetic as the standard answer to the question of why the chicken crossed the road they are rarely as feeble as concealed-environment and concealed-identity questions. Stories of this kind are harder to devise than Shaggy God stories and their kin, and are thus less likely to fall prey to woefully weak endings. There are, however, some common variants of which you need to beware. One involves the silly behaviour of aliens eventually being explained by the fact that they are not adults but infants. The other features a hapless hero who is threatened, harassed and pursued for no apparent reason, until he is told after his eventual capture that it has all been a test to see how he would perform – usually to determine his fitness for acceptance into the social elite.

In trying to set up the 'why' of the story you need to make sure that the explanation of what is going on is sensible, and that the motive forces driving your characters are plausible – but if you can do both these things you should have no trouble gripping your readers.

How?

The 'how' of a story usually follows on from the 'why', being concerned with the plans which the characters formulate in order to carry through their various projects or deal with their various problems. Whereas their motives will remain more or less constant throughout, however, their plans are likely to require continual modification. Advice which you would do well to bear in mind in introducing the how of a story is Robert Burns' observation that 'the best laid schemes o' mice an' men gang aft a-gley'. From the viewpoint of the writer beginning a story – though not, of course, from that of the character – the best schemes are those which are going to come horribly unstuck, thus complicating the plot.

This matter will be discussed in more detail in the next chapter, so it will be sufficient for now to say that any story whose central characters can immediately formulate a plan that will see them safely through to a successful conclusion is bound to seem flat. Whether or not you intend your story to have a climactic twist in the tail it will certainly benefit from having a few unexpected twists and turns in the middle, and the best way to do that is to start the central character off with a plan of campaign that *seems* perfectly reasonable but is fated to go awry.

In beginning your stories you should always bear in mind that some kind of complication will be necessary, and you may well want to prepare the way for it by introducing a deliberate flaw into its make-up.

This requirement is particularly vital in comedy. Comedies often consist of a whole string of carefully – or desperately – formulated plans, each one of which comes so badly unstuck as to make the situation worse instead of better. In thrillers, too, it is often a sensible strategy to force the hero's hastily formulated plans to undergo a series of increasingly desperate adaptations as the situations he encounters become even more complicated or awkward. In beginning a story the one thing that you must *not* set down for your reader's benefit is the exact means by which the end of the story will ultimately be contrived. Ideally, what ought to be set down in its stead is a plausible alternative which will be tried and found wanting as your story gets under way, thus renewing or re-enlivening the initial challenge.

In fantasy and science fiction stories there is another kind of 'how' question which might also require careful thought: the issue of how the future world got to be the way it is, or how it came about that the strange event happened where and when it did.

It has to be admitted that questions of this kind often go unanswered, or are frequently answered in a blatantly tokenistic fashion, using handy all-purpose explanations. 'Radiation' has become a favourite all-purpose explanation in science fiction, accounting for the sudden appearance of countless giant insects, gifted children and eccentrically talented superheroes. This is not surprising, given that radiation is known to cause mutations – thus lending plausibility to the notion that it might generate dramatically-interesting metamorphoses – although the logic of the argument is seriously flawed. Magic spells perform the equivalent function in fantasy, and writers of such stories rarely feel compelled to offer any kind of explanation of *how* they work. Although this might be deemed bad practice by purists, it is worth bearing in mind that if readers are perfectly content with tokenistic explanations you risk boring them if you insist on giving them more.

If you are writing the kind of story that requires you to provide a detailed explanation of how your much-changed future arose out of our own near future, or the kind that compels you to map out the history of your secondary world in great detail, the task is usually best left to a late stage in the narration. This kind of info-dump is the most difficult to leak into a story discreetly because the information has to be organised into a long and fairly coherent sequence. It is almost invariably the case that the best way to handle such weighty masses of information is to conserve them, making puzzles of them where possible and adding extra pieces in a teasing fashion until the reader will be duly grateful for a straightforward lecture putting everything in its proper place.

The beginning and the end

Characters narrating their own stories often start out by saying 'Where shall I begin?' They know that the obvious answer is 'At the beginning' but they also know that it is by no means obvious when and where 'the beginning' actually was. Every person's story might be held to begin at the moment of birth, but even that event is a consequence of a chain of cause-and-effect extending all the way back to the Big Bang (and sometimes, in science fiction, even further).

It would, of course, be ludicrous to expect all stories to begin with the birth of the characters, and very few actually do – although there are exceptions, and Mervyn Peake's *Titus Groan* is entirely concerned with events leading up to the birth of the character for whom the book is named. A narrative usually begins with the significant event with which it is concerned – the 'what' of the story – but if the chain of events which unfolds within the story is unusually complicated it may be very difficult to locate a single crucial event which can be unambiguously unidentified as its point of origin. 'Where shall I begin?' can pose remarkably awkward problems for a narrator – and, of course, for the narrator's creator.

When dealing with short stories, the conventional answer to the question of 'Where shall I begin?' is 'As close to the end as possible'. It is, however, possible to begin a story too close to the end – and this is something that inexperienced writers are often tempted to do. It is perilously easy to write 'static stories' which have no movement of their own at all – a story, for instance, which begins with the protagonist about to commit suicide and ends with the moment of death, with the middle of the story consisting of an explanatory flashback.

Stories of this kind can work well – long novels are sometimes enclosed in spare 'frame narratives' whose beginnings act as teasers – but they can easily become clumsy if the flashback sequence cannot be made to run smoothly. If you set out to write a story like this you might well find yourself bending the enclosed story into a very ungainly shape in order to cram it into the available narrative space.

Any manifest delay in the flow of a narrative is likely to be costly, but simply shifting the delay from the story proper into a flashback will not automatically solve the problem and warping the movement of the story back in time may cause problems of its own. If your story does have to skip a few hours or days, in the interests of getting from start to finish at a reasonably fast and steady pace, it can usually be contrived by discreet use of text breaks: blank lines which signal to the readers that the story has left off at one point in time and is resuming at another.

The punctuation of your narrative with text breaks may compel you to supplement your original beginning with a series of 'mini-beginnings' which explain where and when you are restarting and with what event after each text break, but this is not usually very burdensome. Such punctuation may, of course, also require you to supply a series of 'mini-endings' – preparatory 'punch-lines' which function as narrative hooks making the reader want to read on – but that can be advantageous as well as slightly troublesome.

In general, it is best to start your story with an event which will allow you to follow a reasonably rapid and smooth-flowing sequence of subsequent events to the climactic resolution. If an event which happened twenty years before the opening event of your story is vital to an understanding of what is going on it can be inserted as a flashback at some convenient point but more diffuse information about events prior to the opening of your story is best handled like any other info-dumping project, by leaking it into the plot in neat and economical packages.

When writing short stories it is always a bad idea to introduce your readers to one set of characters and circumstances and then to discard them abruptly in favour of another and more important set. This is, however, much more common practice in novels where an opening prelude can function as a dramatic introduction to themes or problems which will ultimately be central to – although not initially obvious within – a more extensive and slower-moving narrative. If, in writing a novel, you have so many characters and so much explanatory material to introduce that your opening has to be slow it is often a good idea to preface it with a striking episode that is both melodramatic and enigmatic, to reassure your readers that once they have got past the painstaking introductory phase the plot will amply reward their patience.

Some further examples

These are the opening paragraphs of a story called 'The Age of Innocence', which appeared in the June 1995 issue of *Asimov's Science Fiction*:

> Sybil and her best friend Gwenan got their first real sex education when they were eleven years old, watching their great-great-great-great-grandparents playing in the park.
>
> The park had several dense clumps of bushes whose principal *raison d'être* was to provide cover for frolicking ancients. Most of the carers who took ancients out to play were adults, who almost invariably made a big show of staying out of the bushes while their charges got on with it, but Sybil and Gwenan were curious enough to take the first reasonable opportunity to slip into the bushes unobserved and find out what went on there.
>
> They were not entirely *surprised*, but the visible reality of sexual intercourse seemed much more absurd than the theory had implied.
>
> 'Surely our *parents* don't do things like that?' said Gwenan, in hushed tones, the first time they saw it happen.
>
> 'Not *now*,' Sybil informed her, airily, taking her customary pride in the narrow margin of her greater wisdom. 'People lose the urge when they get to be a hundred or so. That's why the second century is supposed to be the prime of life – all their creativity can be concentrated in *useful* channels. It only comes back again when the higher brain functions begin to disappear, and by the time they get to three

hundred or three-fifty they're slaves to it. I heard Mother say so, when she was talking on the phone to Aunt Genista.'

Gwenan became embarrassed then, and turned away, but Sybil didn't. It wasn't that she didn't feel awkward spying on them, just that her curiosity was stronger than her guilty unease. All sorts of questions ran through her head. Were ancients capable of loving one another, after their fashion, or did love vanish along with self-consciousness – and if it did, could they even be said to love their descendants? Would ancients have sex with *anybody* – anybody, that is, who was small enough – or did they prefer particular partners? *Why* did ancients like sex so much, given that they were quite incapable of procreation? *Did* they actually like it, or was it just a kind of compulsion?

The title of the story is, of course, a prelude of sorts to the opening paragraphs. Like many science-fictional titles this one is calculatedly deceptive; it echoes the double-meaning of the title of Edith Wharton's famous novel ('age' referring to childhood and to a particular era of history) but adds a third element; in the world of *this* story, the 'second childhood' of old age has been much extended.

The 'who' of the story is introduced forthrightly in paragraph one, the slightly exotic names displacing the narrative a little, but not too far, from the familiar. The 'when' and the 'where' are left rather vague but the references to a much-extended lifespan place it in a fairly distant future and the fact that there is a park with bushes creates the (correct) impression that the location is not particularly exotic – thus allowing any Anglo-American reader to read it as if it has a local setting.

The 'what' of the story is the set of social adaptations necessitated by biotechnological innovations which have allowed the human lifespan to be extended in this slightly problematic manner, and the opening dialogue serves to get the basic situation across while bringing a little more definition to the two central characters.

The 'why' of the story is the girls' embarrassed curiosity about the unashamed sexual exploits of their ancestors, although the first section of the story goes on to end with an abrupt shift in this preliminary pattern – Sybil's great-great-great-great-grandmother is killed in a road accident, so that she must supplement her new acquaintance with the reality of sex with a similar acquaintance with the reality of death.

The 'how' of the story is uncomplicated, as befits a short (5,000 words) 'slice-of-life' piece. The opening paragraphs establish that Sybil is attempting – with some uncertainty – to follow the conventional course of education with which her care of the family ancient is supposed to provide her. Her initial resentment of the impositions of her role is later to be confused by guilt and grief – and the expected sentiments which she sets out dutifully to fake eventually become real as she observes the uncomprehending reaction to her own ancestor's death of Gwenan's great-great-great-great grandfather.

These are the opening paragraphs of a fantasy story called 'The Evil That Men Do', which appeared in the August 1995 issue of *Realms of Fantasy*.

The crimson sands of the Cinnabar Desert had always had a mysterious attraction for eremites and cenobites alike. While the cenobites laboured long and hard to ring its deep-set wells with stern edifices of stone and sun-baked brick, the eremites found homes among the caves that pitted the vermilion cliffs, which had been weathered for thousands of years by the simoom which blew from the west.

These holy men served half a hundred different gods, and competed fiercely with one another, on behalf of their solemn masters, to set the most perfect examples of chastity, austerity, humility and self-mortification. There was not a man among them who did not dress himself in a bug-infested hair-shirt by day and lie down upon the cold bare rock by night. None ever slept for longer than an hour,

---

and all but the feeblest in body and soul scourged themselves thrice daily with nettles, thorns or supple rods according to their taste. The hardiest of them were ever-eager to inflict themselves with purulent ulcers and festering sores, for their gods were of the uncompromising kind which had put their followers on earth to win purity of spirit by tormenting the flesh; the few old men among them went naked but for their loincloths, in order to show their younger brethren what a beautiful mass of livid scar-tissue a human body might become, with the proper encouragement.

Although they had sought refuge in the Cinnabar Desert in order that they should be as far away as it was possible to be from those sinks of iniquity which men called cities, the eremites and cenobites were by no means free from temptation, for the region drew imps and succubi and all manner of other petty demons like a magnet, whose delight was to taunt these happy and innocent folk with terrible nightmares. By day, the Cinnabar Desert was the most desolate place imaginable, but by night it became a battlefield where the forces of Light and Dark fought bitter skirmishes in memory of that long-ago battle which was supposed to have settled such questions forever. But the cenobites and eremites quickly became so hardy that no temptation could shake their resolve.

There was no better place in all the world for the souls of men to be purified. There never was a sinner so great that he could not be turned into a man of indomitable virtue by the fierce heat of the desert sun.

This is a more leisurely opening than the previous example, the story being 11,000 words long. The central character has not yet been mentioned specifically, although the work done so far paves the way for his introduction as the holiest of all these supposedly holy men. The 'when' of the story is necessarily vague by comparison with the where – which is described in calculatedly ornate language that serves as a distancing device – although the third paragraph takes care to mention that it is a world where moral issues have supposedly been settled by some kind of apocalyptic event.

The 'what' of the story will be the protagonist's quest to expiate the sins he committed before becoming an eremite, but the blatant sarcasm of the paragraphs above serve to establish that the 'why' and the 'how' – his motives and his methods – are both suspect, to be regarded with extreme scepticism. At the end of the story the protagonist will achieve *exactly* what he sets out to achieve – but what he sees as a triumph will be revealed by the objective viewpoint to be a terrible disaster, thus illustrating the unfortunate fact that the people with the most fervent determination to do good often end up doing terrible harm.

3

THE YELLOW BRICK ROAD: PLOTS

What is a plot?

A plot is what connects the beginning of a story to its end. When writers talk about plotting they usually do so in terms of a plot *structure*. A common metaphor speaks of plot 'threads', imagining that such threads intertwine within a story to form a kind of rope that will draw the reader through the story.

It is not necessary for every story to have a sturdy plot. Short stories of the 'slice-of-life' variety and 'mood pieces' can often get by with only the merest shadow of a plot structure. You need to remember, however, that what makes most stories interesting to most readers is their plots. You need to make some provision to draw your reader through your work, and a good plot has the kind of pulling power which makes it easier to do that. If you try to get by with a weak plot – or if your plot loses its momentum – your story will lose its grip on at least some readers.

Plot structures may be sliced up for analysis in several different ways but the simplest way to begin an examination of plot anatomy is to divide each individual thread into three phases – challenge, complication and climax – and then examine the different ways in which threads can be gathered together to increase their pulling power.

Challenges

The necessities of life lay down the basic pattern of challenges which can be set out in a plot. At its most basic, life is a matter of survival and reproduction, and there is a sense in which almost all plots can be reduced to these matters. However calm and well-ordered it is, life presents itself to us as an endless flow of threats and opportunities affecting our fortunes in the lottery of well-being, and these threats and opportunities determine the kinds of challenges which can be used to launch and sustain plots.

Survival is, of course, more than the avoidance of death; it includes everything involved in 'making a living'. Any matter of considerable relevance to a character's livelihood poses a challenge, and there are certain jobs – policeman, journalist, spy, etc – which routinely present their holders with an endless series of problems; this is why these professions tend to be much more prominent in the worlds within texts than they are in the real world. The routines of making a living exist under constant threat of disruption and termination, but they also throw up opportunities for enrichment and enlightenment. Such opportunities may also present challenges which can drive a plot; treasure-hunting has always been a popular pastime in fiction.

Reproduction is important as a source of challenges by courtesy of the preliminaries which lead up to it and the confusions which subsequently beset it. The forces of sexual attraction, sexual jealousy and parental affection are powerful in life and even more powerful in fiction. As with making a living, the business of selecting and holding on to sexual partners is constantly subject to the threat of failure, but it also provides a flow of new opportunities. Children, in fiction as in life, are a constant source of worry and wonder.

There is a sense in which fantasy and science fiction writers are bound by exactly the same spectrum of challenges as writers of known-world fiction. No matter how outlandish your story may be, your characters will still be faced with the same fundamental problems of survival and reproduction. The particular threats which your characters are likely to face may include dragons, magical attacks, alien invasions and new plagues but they still function within your plots as threats. Fairy-tale princesses often face difficulties in obtaining a husband that ordinary women rarely encounter, and science-fictional futures may involve new and peculiar reproductive systems, but no matter what changes have overtaken the worlds within your texts you will be relying on the same fundamental motive forces to get your plots moving. There is, however, one kind of challenge which is much more important in fantasy and science fiction than it is in known world fiction, and that is the challenge of the unknown.

The challenge of the unknown is an ever-present aspect of the business of survival. Everyday life constantly thrusts us into new situations and we all know perfectly well how stressful it can be when we are unsure how to behave in situations we have never been in before. Nor are such known-world unknowns restricted to matters of personal ignorance; the real world is subject to a constant flow of innovations and would be even if technological progress were far less rapid. In fantasy and science fiction stories, the challenge of the unknown becomes a much more active and extravagant force than it is in life or known-world fiction, with the consequence that both genres readily lend themselves to the cultivation of horror and a sense of wonder.

The jolts which are delivered to characters in known-world fiction in order to set plots in motion may be brutal, and the particular characters involved may be totally unprepared to face them, but they are never truly *alien*. By contrast, fantasy and science fiction plots are often kick-started by confronting the characters with objects or situations which they have previously considered impossible – and the fact that the characters are compelled to reappraise the limits of possibility may well be the most important aspect of the challenge presented to them. Because of this, the task facing you, as a writer of fantasy or science fiction, is not simply to come up with challenges to set before your characters but also to heighten and dramatise the extra dimension of the challenge of the unknown.

Fortunately, this is something which fascinates large numbers of potential readers. There are plenty of people in the world so avid to face the challenge of the unknown that they will go to extraordinary lengths to do it, valiantly risking the ridicule which inevitably attaches to people who think they have actually seen ghosts, remembered previous existences or been abducted by aliens.

Complications

Challenges which are too easily met and overcome are essentially uninteresting. Even in real life we routinely exaggerate the difficulties which we have faced in the interests of making ourselves seem more heroic and our lives more dramatic. Victories always seem more worthwhile if they are hard-won, and failure is easier to bear if we have the compensation of knowing that the one that got away was no run-of-the-mill tiddler. Once you have launched your characters into a plot, therefore, there is much to be gained by increasing the difficulties with which they must contend.

You can complicate a plot simply by arranging matters so that each individual challenge your characters meet and overcome is swiftly followed by another. This can be done simply by placing a series of traps and opportunities along the course which your characters have to follow, so that your plot resembles a game of snakes-and-ladders. If you are clever, though, you might be able to arrange matters so that a solution to the initial problem actually generates a bigger problem, whose solution generates a bigger one still. Such a pattern exerts a more powerful pull than one in which each difficulty is overcome, and each opportunity taken, as its turn arises.

Patterns of this escalating kind have a certain innate fascination, as exhibited by the song about the woman who accidentally swallowed a fly, then swallowed a spider to catch the fly, then swallowed a bird to catch the spider, and so on. Computer games are usually designed with a hierarchy of levels so that the more skilled the players become in managing the game's 'central character' the stiffer are the challenges they have to meet. If each challenge your characters meet and overcome serves to draw them into further and greater difficulties the dramatic tension of your plot will increase inexorably.

There are, of course, more ingenious ways to increase complication by increasing complexity. A favourite method involves disguising the true nature and magnitude of the challenge which faces your characters, so that it changes as they find out more about it. If you can present a challenge in such a way that it seems relatively trivial at first, revealing its true dimensions by slow degrees, you will obtain the same kind of escalator effect as a multi-levelled computer game in a neater way. This is usually easier to arrange when using threats as challenges – it is a standard pattern in thrillers and horror stories, where the manifestations of the criminal conspiracy or the supernatural agency usually become increasingly insistent and increasingly nasty. A similar pattern using an opportunistic kind of challenge is standardised in science-fictional mysteries, where a research scientist who notices a tiny anomaly in his experimental results may be led thereby to the step-by-step disclosure of something truly awesome.

Complication, especially when it is ingeniously contrived, is sometimes known as 'thickening' the plot. The thickening in question is the increased resistance your characters face as they find that matters are much more convoluted than they thought and that the goals they have in mind will be much more difficult to reach.

Fantasy and science fiction writers have more abundant opportunities to thicken plots than writers of known-world fiction. The complexity of a fantastic device is something which you can extend at will, although you will have to make sure that the idea remains reasonably coherent. Supplementary magical objects and new discoveries can be thrown into a plot at any time and stirred into the mix. This is so easy, in fact, that writers of fantasy and science fiction are sometimes inclined to use a 'mixing-bowl' method of plotting which involves throwing all the ideas they happen to have in store into their current story and allowing them to interact with one another. Even when the result is a sticky and unresolved mess it can be quirkily appetising, provided that the initial ingredients were sufficiently toothsome. Not all plots are made according to strict recipes, nor do all plots have to be.

Complication by continued and haphazard innovation has its problems as well as its advantages. A plot which becomes too complicated is apt to leave numerous 'loose ends' when its main threads reach their resolution. However, although loose ends are untidy and may annoy readers, it is often better to leave a few loose ends dangling than to make do with a plot that does not have enough threads to generate any real pulling power.

If you can come up with enough interesting ideas with which to stock the worlds within your texts, and enough ways to make them challenging, you will usually be able to pull your readers along with ease.

You can mix threatening and alluring possibilities with reckless abandon, and you do not have to resolve every single challenge to produce an ending which will pass muster, but you risk losing the sympathy of your readers if you do not think your ideas *through*.

One thing to beware of when casually throwing ideas into your plot is 'using a sledgehammer to crack a nut' – that is to say, using a big idea to present a little challenge while utterly neglecting its wider implications. There are whole sub-genres of fantastic fiction which routinely do this – horror stories often invoke entities with godlike powers to pester the characters with a series of petty practical jokes, without ever giving much thought to the wider implications of their existence – but you will earn the respect of more discriminating readers if you are more careful.

There are, of course, many fantasy novels in which magic is invoked solely to do what the plot requires, and has effects which are exactly tailored to the requirement of each individual dramatic moment. You ought, however, to be willing to examine your inventions carefully as they crop up, to see whether all the likely applications of the spells they display have been considered, and whether the characters are doing something *now* which – had you only thought of it at the time – could have got them out of an earlier predicament which they solved by some more laborious means. This is even more necessary in science fiction stories, which are supposed to be rigorous in their extrapolation of the ideas they use.

Although this aspect of creativity can be difficult it can also be rewarding. It is always worth trying to figure out exactly what the implications of your ideas are, not only because you might be able to work out better ways to thicken your current plot, but also because you will almost certainly discover alternative challenges that may be held in reserve for use in future stories.

Climaxes

The complications of your plot must eventually precipitate some kind of crisis which demands resolution. The dramatic tension which you have been building up slowly and inexorably must be released far more quickly, if not explosively. In this respect – as the use of the term 'climax' implies – good plotting resembles good sex.

The simplest way of building dramatic tension to a climax is to make your characters work against the clock, so that they come closer and closer to a deadline at which everything must be settled. Michael Moorcock has said that his early fantasy novels mostly followed a formula he describes as 'six days to save the world', exploiting the fact that as the countdown continued from six days to one the urgency of the character's actions inevitably increased. Thrillers of all kinds frequently make use of countdowns in their climaxes, and those which feature high 'body counts' often involve a countdown of characters by which a group under threat will be whittled down until only one or two survive.

Another way to precipitate a climax is to introduce an event which serves as a 'catalyst' or 'seed crystal' which abruptly puts the complications of the plot into a different perspective, giving matters which had not previously seemed pressing a sudden urgency. This may involve shifting your central characters out of the plan they have been following, forcing them to flee or fight. In climaxes of this kind the apparent timetable of the plot is rudely shattered, so that its tacit countdown takes a great leap forward.

Several abrupt changes of context may be introduced at intervals, so that a series of 'sub-climaxes' lead up to the ultimate climax, each one greater in magnitude than the last. If you are clever, you may be able to arrange your plot in such a way that a whole series of surprises lie in wait for your readers, so that each narrative ambush follows hot on the heels of another. This is a particularly attractive option in fantasy and science fiction because these genres rely so heavily on ideas and innovations. If you decide to construct a series of sub-climaxes, however, you will need to conserve your best ammunition for your final ambush; a climax that is upstaged by its preliminary sub-climaxes is bound to seem weak.

The art of engineering climaxes is in the build-up rather than the resolution. The effect of your ending will depend on the force of the climax which precedes it; the more dramatic tension you create, the more impact its release will generate. In countdown plots this can be done by letting the countdown run to the last minute, or even the last second, but such brinkmanship works much better in visual media like film and TV where the camera can keep cutting to a flickering digital display or a sweeping second-hand. Interrupting a text with a continual flow of numbers is less elegant, and it is usually convenient to find other ways of indicating the intensity of the pressure that your characters are under. On the other hand, a text can describe the psychological states of the characters as their thoughts and emotions come under increasing stress.

One of the most attractive features of fantasy and science fiction, to readers and writers, is that climaxes can carry a much greater load than in another genres. This makes for easy satirisation, such phrases as 'the end of the world as we know it' having been devalued by overuse, but it remains a great asset to the writer of fantastic fiction that the fate of the whole world – or of the entire universe – may hang in the balance when the climax arrives. Fantasy often makes possible a final settling of the moral account books as the evil-personifying Dark Lord comes to the very brink of victory before being thwarted. In science fiction, planets may explode and the 'fabric of space-time' may be unceremoniously ripped apart in the interests of overcoming suitably extreme threats. Many fantasy and science fiction stories are, of course, much humbler in their aspiration, dealing with matters of purely personal concern, but even in the tiniest application of magic or advanced science there is a promise of so much more, and clever writers use this promise to give their climaxes extra weight.

A climax is, of course, what brings a story to its ending – just as a challenge is what carries it away from its beginning – but there are good reasons for discussing endings in a separate chapter. One is that although climaxes may fuse with endings in stories which conclude very abruptly – as those which end with a 'twist in the tail' often do – most stories actually extend some way beyond their climaxes.

The extension of a story beyond its climax can produce a let-down effect and the management of such extensions can pose awkward tactical problems for the writer. If the climax of your story happens in some remote arena from which a long and laborious return is necessary before a proper conclusion is in place you may need to keep a little narrative drive in reserve. In fantasy and science fiction it is frequently the case that the climax will occur in an exotic location, while the ending must wait until the characters have come home again.

A common method of coping with this problem is to skip over the intervening time and space – even when the homeward journeys are difficult and fraught with peril – in a few brief paragraphs, or with the aid of a text break. This has the effect of condensing the ending of a story into an 'epilogue' whose disconnection from the flow of the narrative may seem crude and unsatisfactory. It is worth remembering that leaping abruptly from climax to ending is not compulsory; Tolkien's *Lord of the Rings* is a notable example of a story which refuses to do so, concluding with an extended epilogue which carefully examines all the different aspects of the aftermath of the climactic battle.

Linear plots

The simplest kind of plot is a journey broken down into stages. The individual threads of such a plot are the various purposes and ambitions of the travelling companions, interwoven by the relationships that form between them – although the simplest versions of such plots make do with a single main character and the unsupported thread of his particular project.

The prototype of all journey plots is Homer's *Odyssey*. After the fall of Troy, Odysseus wants to go home, but his ship is continually blown off course and his homeward journey is delayed by a sequence of exotic encounters. Many a subsequent story has done no more, although most writers borrowing Homer's plot have taken note of the fact that it does have a significant sub-plot which introduces a climactically useful countdown. As time goes by, the hero's patient wife Penelope finds it more and more difficult to stave off the demands made by her suitors.

The odyssey is still the basic plot-form of genre fantasy, although the journey is usually reconfigured as an expedition from home rather than an attempt to return, thus becoming a *quest*. Heroic fantasy of the 'wandering barbarian' variety is usually content to present its central characters with a series of arbitrary threats and adventures, but most secondary-world fantasy is very earnest, investing the characters' quests with much greater moral significance.

Much of the apparatus of the modern fantasy genre can be traced back to the chivalric romances of medieval times, which glorified the feudal system of social organisation. In romances of that kind the adventures of knights errant – usually involving remarkable feats of arms, the slaying of dragons, the rescuing of damsels in distress, and so on – had to be combined with Christian ideals, and the most convenient way of doing that was to introduce a sacred but essentially unobtainable goal which would give the knights' peregrinations a purpose. The Holy Grail was drafted to play this part. (Exaggerated earnestness inevitably invites mockery, so it is not entirely surprising that just as the excesses of medieval romance were satirised by *Don Quixote*, so the re-establishment of quest fantasy as a popular genre in the 1970s was followed in the 1980s by the subversive humour of Terry Pratchett.)

The fundamental attraction of an odyssey plot is that it can be literally mapped out. You can simply draw up a list of interesting places where dramatic encounters can take place and send your characters forth to follow a set of instructions. If you like, you can even lay down a guideline for them, as L. Frank Baum did for Dorothy in Oz, when he set the Emerald City at the far end of the Yellow Brick Road. At its most basic, plotting consists of designing interesting stop off points and laying dramatic ambushes along a (usually invisible) yellow brick road. One of the advantages which secondary-world fantasy has over historical fantasy is that the grail-substitute which awaits the characters at the end of the road can actually be reached and used to change the world.

This kind of plotting is so amenable to formularisation that it is employed as the basic format of fantasy role-playing games like *Dungeons and Dragons* and *Warhammer*. The ease with which such plots can be reduced to recipes has been satirised by Nick Lowe, who provided a scathing analysis of stories in which heroes trudge from point to point across a map collecting a series of 'plot coupons', so that when they have the full set they can send them off to the author in exchange for an apocalypse. The same article also points out the extreme convenience of such devices as the 'get-out-of-jail-free card', whereby the hero acquires an extra magical object whose power and significance he does not understand but which will eventually turn out to be exactly what he needs to get out of an uncomfortably tight corner.

Actually, the fact that odyssey plots are so common in fantasy and science fiction is not a reflection of the laziness or simple-mindedness of writers working in those genres. In any story which does not use known-world settings the world within the text has to be *invented*, and the more exotic that world is the more work the writer has to do in constructing its geography, its history and its ecology. This work has to be made clear to the reader somehow, and by far the most convenient way of doing it is to send the characters forth on a journey that will cover a good deal of the geography, introduce them to various relics of the history and allow them to observe the interactions of local plants and animals. Even if a fantasy plot does not consist entirely of a journey, therefore, it often makes good sense to include a substantial journey somewhere within it.

The necessity of providing elaborate descriptions of certain worlds within texts means that although odyssey plots may be simple, and may be planned out with relative ease, they may also require a good deal of painstaking fine-tuning. Counting down the number of days your characters have to collect their plot coupons and save the world can become a troublesome business when every sideways glance and every chance remark has to communicate information to the reader regarding the nature of the world they are trying to save. One of the reasons why fantasies are often designed as trilogies is that the second volume of three (which has, by definition, neither beginning nor end) offers a convenient space for an info-dumping odyssey.

Plots and counterplots

The simplest way to complicate an odyssey plot is to split it into two threads and alternate the segments. The company of characters you initially send forth on their quest can be quickly divided into two or three, and the sub-units can be kept apart until the climax. The adventures of the various groups can be told in alternating chapters, allowing the text breaks which bridge the parts of each journey where nothing much happens to be filled in with solid narrative meat. When the climax arrives the groups can be reunited, pooling all the dramatic tension they have separately accumulated. This is, of course, the method employed by *The Lord of the Rings* and most of the works that followed in its wake. Contemporary editors tend to regard it as the best template for use in concocting best-selling action-adventure stories.

The great advantage of the kind of plot structure which lays out two threads in an alternating pattern is that it allows you to increase narrative tension considerably. You can not only fill in text breaks which would otherwise break up the flow of your story but you can actually increase the force of that flow by ending chapters with 'narrative hooks'. Instead of bringing each chapter to a 'mini-ending' you bring it to a point at which your characters have just been confronted with a *new* challenge and leave them in that predicament while you revert to the alternative cast, to explain how they escaped from the awkward situation to which *they* were abandoned and delivering them to another just as acute.

The melodramatic chapter endings employed in this kind of pattern are often referred to as 'cliff-hangers' and their use was taken to extremes by such cinematic serials as *Flash Gordon*, in which concluding footage which strongly implied that the characters were doomed was routinely replaced in the next episode with re-edited footage which left scope for their salvation. When two such narrative threads alternate with mechanical regularity they are sometimes described as plot and counterplot.

If you maintain this kind of plot/counterplot pattern throughout a novel you can keep your readers permanently 'in suspense'. Whatever is resolved within a chapter there can always be another problem waiting in the wings. It is not necessary to end every chapter with a full-blown cliff-hanger – and it may be politic to save the really nasty predicaments for the crisis preceding the climax so as to obtain a crescendo effect – but any kind of teaser which will make your readers want to race through the intervening chapter in order to find out what happened next will increase the pulling power of your plot. Double-stranded plots can be useful in short fiction too. Merging the different agendas which two characters are following – especially if the merging produces consequences that neither party desired or anticipated – is one of the standard methods of constructing twist-in-the-tail endings.

Alternation is not the only way to double up a narrative. At its most elementary, the doubled-up format is reducible to a single flashback within a 'frame narrative'. The advantage of this structure is that you can set out a teasing problem or a puzzling situation which remains in suspense while you painstakingly fill in the background to that state of affairs. If you are writing the kind of story which requires a beginning somewhat distant from its end it is usually convenient to arrange this kind of 'fold', so that the slow part of your narrative can be suspended between two more dramatic parts. Returning to a previously established frame can also excuse the abrupt leap from climax to ending which remotely set climaxes sometimes require; epilogues often seem more apt when they are paired with prologues.

The most artful use of plot/counterplot doubling usually involves setting up some kind of parallel process within the two strands. There is a sub-genre of fantasy that interweaves stories which are set in different periods of history but involve some common object or theme. Alan Garner's *Red Shift* is one of the most notable recent examples. It has often been observed that history tends to repeat itself, especially if the actors involved have not learned lessons laid down for them by the previous cycles.

Such repetitions often form a key element of tragedy, because the idea of tragedy is closely connected to the ideas of destiny and fate. A reader's sense of tragedy can be considerably heightened by the implication that the trap awaiting the characters is one which constantly and malevolently lies in wait for everyone. You can often increase the tension of a present-day narrative by comparing it with a past sequence of events which ended disastrously, partly because the completed sequence emphasises the threat which your contemporary characters must avoid, and partly because the suggestion that the end is 'fated' will add extra tension to your climax. For this reason, the effect of a plot and counterplot working in harness may be much greater than the sum of their parts.

Multi-stranded plots

Long novels often complicate the plot/counterplot structure by employing three or even four alternating narrative threads. This can become awkward, because leaving your readers in suspense for too long may make them impatient; they are less likely to increase their pace to find out what happened next in one sequence if they know that they will have to read two or three intervening chapters before they can find out. The multi-stranded plot is, however, uniquely useful in some kinds of story, including some kinds widely represented in fantasy and science fiction. The most obvious example is provided by disaster stories.

By definition, a disaster is something that happens to a lot of people and it therefore makes perfect sense if you are writing a disaster story to use a lot of characters. There is a certain poignancy already built in to the fact that the passengers on a ship or plane which strays into some kind of strange and dangerous situation may form a crude cross-section of society, exemplifying many different reasons for taking that particular journey at that particular time and embodying a whole fleet of representative personal problems. The awful magnitude of a natural disaster which threatens a town or a whole world can only be conveyed by showing its effect on several different people scattered over a wide area.

It is neither necessary nor desirable to run all the viewpoints within a disaster story in strict rotation but it is often politic to set up a number of different viewpoints to which you can remove your ongoing narrative as and when it becomes convenient. Whenever you are dealing with large-scale events in a story – as you will often have to do if you take advantage of the scope which fantasy and science fiction offer for grandiose climaxes – you will probably want to reveal those events by degrees and track their progress carefully. You will find it very convenient, therefore, to plant characters at a whole series of useful vantage points. In the interests of dramatic tension it is advisable to equip all these characters with goals and agendas of their own, so that they are more than mere reporters slotting info-dumps into your plot.

Managing multi-stranded plots can become frustratingly difficult. (Anyone can juggle two balls, but juggling four or five requires much greater skill.) Some writers prefer to write each strand separately and then shuffle them all together, moving the pieces around until they arrive at a pattern which maximises the ease of narrative flow, then filling in extra bridging pieces where required. The main problem associated with this method is that even if the plot-threads are entirely separate from one another – and they rarely are, because tangled threads are usually more interesting – it may be awkward to fit them neatly into the same time-frame. If the plot-strands have to make occasional contact with one another, briefly touching as characters meet and interact, fitting them together into a coherent and smoothly flowing whole can become very difficult indeed.

Given that stories of the multi-stranded kind tend to be long and that all stories mutate as they grow, it is probably sensible to switch back and forth between narrative threads as you write, even if you still have to do a certain amount of shuffling to get the bits into the best order. My most extensive adventure of this kind – a 560,000-word epic called *Genesys*, published in three volumes, was written in this fashion. The most difficult part of the task was trying to fit the various threads into the same time-frame in such a way as to permit a reasonably dramatic alternation of chapters, so I tried to follow each group through a fixed period – usually a few days – and then slice up each narrative into an appropriate number of units; the result was rarely as neat as I would wish but I hope the final product is not too uneven.

One of the great advantages of a multi-stranded plot is that you can drop various kinds of 'vignettes' into the overall pattern. Info-dumps of all kinds are easier to insert into a multi-stranded plot than a linear one because it is by nature a thing of fits and starts. At its most extreme, the multi-stranded plot may become 'kaleidoscopic', building up an image of the world within the text by means of a 'narrative collage'. The American novelist John Dos Passos developed a literary method of this kind which was adopted into science fiction by John Brunner in the classic *Stand on Zanzibar*, which supplements numerous narrative threads – many of which are deliberately left hanging loose – with all kinds of peripheral texts-within-texts: news broadcasts, quotes from imaginary books, graffiti, snippets of over-heard conversation, and so forth.

These kinds of narrative special effects can easily become so over-whelming as to deter some readers, but readers who can cope with the information overload may feel that they have got a much better grip on the world within the text than any linear narrative or simple alter-nation of plot and counterplot could ever have permitted. Designing a multi-stranded plot is the only real alternative to sending your char-acters on a long journey if the world within your text needs to be described in considerable detail.

Originality

There are some plots which can be repeated in all their essential features without offending readers. Indeed, there are whole genres of fiction which employ formulaic plot-patterns in which only a few details need to be changed in order to import the necessary degree of difference which makes each text 'new'. Writers active in such genres can, if they wish, write what is effectively 'the same story' over and over again.

Within the fantasy genre there are sub-genres of this type – many quest stories are effectively carbon copies of one another and there are imitations of *The Lord of the Rings* which sail very close to the line of propriety that separates pastiche from plagiarism. Within both fantasy and science fiction, however, there are sub-genres which place a very heavy emphasis on novelty and originality.

'Idea as hero' stories make their principal appeal to the reader on the grounds that they are doing something which is both new and clever. Writers setting out on careers in fantasy and science fiction often find this demand for novelty intimidating, although happening upon what seems to be a good idea for a story is what first fires their interest in writing. I suspect that many of the people who have set out to read this book have done so because they already have an idea for a story that they are enthusiastic to develop.

Anxious writers may take some reassurance from the fact that a single good idea may generate a whole series of plots. Once Isaac

Asimov had worked out the three laws of robotics they provided him with a reasonably steady flow of interesting plots for the rest of his life – and other writers were able to pick up the central theme and work out their own variants, as Jack Williamson did in the classic 'With Folded Hands'. When Bob Shaw first thought of slow glass it took him two years to figure out the plot which would display the idea to its best advantage – but then he was able to devise fascinating challenges that the invention might pose to different people in different situations.

Novelty is something that can only arise against a background of familiarity. Most 'new' plots are, in fact, old plots with a single significant variation and one of the most fascinating aspects of fantasy and science fiction is that novums *evolve* as writers borrow ideas from one another, in order to take them one step further or to offer contradictory accounts of the implications they contain. This means that writers interested in producing state-of-the-art fantasy and science fiction need to be reasonably well-read in their genre, but it also means that writers who are well-read have abundant resources available to them in the form of idea-based plots which need only to be nudged in a slightly different direction or mixed with one additional ingredient to become interestingly original.

For example, there is a sub-genre of fantasy in which the characters suffer an exchange of identities, as in the oft-filmed book *Vice Versa* by F. Anstey. In the original version a man exchanges identities with his young son, and learns that the conventional assurances he has been giving the boy about schooldays being the happiest days of one's life are ludicrously mistaken. That particular pattern of exchange has been re-explored, especially in the more recent film versions, but the more interesting variations on *Vice Versa*'s theme are those which substitute characters in different relationships. There are versions in which employers exchange identities with servants, rich men with poor, black men with white, mothers with daughters, husbands with wives, and so on. Some of these tales are merely poor imitations of the original, but the great majority succeed in adding an extra dimension of interest to the basic idea. The question which is the driving force of all such stories – what if you could change places with someone you envy or pity or hate? – is one which can retain its pulling power through a whole series of individual cases. Like any good hero, a strong idea can sustain any number of individual idea-as-hero stories.

Some writers, in setting out to produce idea-as-hero stories, take care to desist from reading other stories that have used similar ideas in case they become subject to too strong an influence. They worry about the possibility that once they have become used to the ideas being worked out in whichever way has become conventional they will find it more difficult to take up a fresh viewpoint. There is some merit in this strategy, because known examples can begin to function as 'paradigm cases' guiding thought into particular channels. There is, however, also a danger that refusing to look at other uses of an idea may lead you to develop a plot-line which someone else has not only anticipated but contrived more cleverly. As Oscar Wilde pointed out, producing a copy of a flower which has more gorgeous petals than the original can be legitimately regarded as a triumph, but producing one which has less merely looks foolish.

The big winners in the game of variations-upon-a-theme are those writers who can familiarise themselves with all extant examples without prejudicing their talent for lateral thinking, but those of us who cannot aspire to such all-round competence have to decide which is the lesser of two evils. Personally, I have always been a voracious reader and would find it very inconvenient to refrain from reading texts which use ideas I might some day want to explore in my writing, but I can easily sympathise with writers who take a different point of view. I am continually tempted to write stories that make elaborate references to works by other writers, which some readers find obscure.

There is, of course, no need to employ the same strategy all the time. If you want to write a story employing a well-used novum like a robot or a vampire the danger of accidentally duplicating moves already made – and perhaps done to death – by other writers is probably greater than the danger of polluting your mind with unwanted influences. On the other hand, if you are dealing with less fashionable materials it may be that the freshness of your approach is an asset to be conserved.

The danger of producing idea-as-hero stories which look weak because they merely reproduce what has been done before is particularly acute in science fiction. This is because science fiction attempts to distinguish itself from 'pure' fantasy by asserting that the ideas established in its 'what if?' stories are licensed by scientific theory as real possibilities, and that their development within the story proceeds on rigorously logical grounds. Different writers developing the same idea are therefore more liable to follow identical chains of reasoning than writers deploying fantastic motifs – or so one might suppose.

Fortunately, different science fiction writers often come up with radically different accounts of the consequences that would follow a particular discovery or invention, and there is usually scope for fierce disagreement as to which chain of reasoning is right. The danger of looking like a fool because you have failed to consider some perfectly reasonable consequence of your central idea is less acute than it seems, and if you are clever you may well be able to find a way to pick holes in the arguments deployed in stories that already exist. For instance, Damon Knight's story 'A for Anything' (1957), which proposes that the invention of a matter-duplicator would cause the economic order of society to collapse, was followed in 1958 by Ralph Williams's 'Business as Usual During Alterations', which carefully argues that such an outcome would not be inevitable.

If you do feel that it would be a good idea to research a theme before using it in a story of your own it can usually be done fairly economically. It isn't actually necessary to read lots of stories about robots to get a reasonable sense of what has already been done with the idea. You can always go to the *Encyclopedia of Science Fiction* and look up the entry on robots; that will give you a thumbnail sketch of the history of the idea and the ways in which authors have developed it.

Troubleshooting

When stories run into difficulties the fault usually lies with the plot. You may get stuck because you don't know what should happen next or you may lose motivation because the story has lost its impetus. Complicated plots have an unfortunate tendency to become so tangled that they develop inextricable knots, while simple ones tend to run out of narrative energy.

In an ideal world we would always be able to avert such problems at the design stage, but no matter how comprehensively you plan a story it still has to grow in the writing, and while it grows it is bound to develop extra features that were not included in your initial outline. As you flesh out the characters their behaviour acquires patterns that may begin to diverge from the set of actions specified in the plot. As you extrapolate the ideas in your story you will discover additional consequences that you hadn't previously noticed. As you get involved in the writing, new ideas may spring into your mind which are far too good to leave out simply because your original plan didn't leave room for them.

All this, of course, assumes that you actually do begin with a fully-worked out plan. Many writers prefer not to do that, and even those who work that way tend to map out the opening phases of their stories in far more detail than the later phases, because they are well aware of all the factors that may force the story-line to diverge from even the best-laid plan. All writers, therefore, need to have some kind of strategy for writing themselves out of difficulty when they run into trouble.

If the story is flagging the sensible thing to do is to make something happen. Raymond Chandler once remarked that if he ever got to a point where he didn't know what was supposed to happen next he had a man come in holding a gun – and then began to figure out who he might be and what he might want. In order to make use of this partic-ular narrative move, however, you have to be writing the kind of story that can never have too many men with guns, and the kind of story that can stand a lot of complication. (An equally famous Chandler anecdote concerns the long discussion between the director and the various scriptwriters at the first screening of *The Big Sleep*, when it turned out that none of them – including Chandler – had the slightest idea who had killed the chauffeur, or why.) The trick is to work out what kind of event is best suited to your particular story and then create it.

When making things happen it is usually a good idea to make them happen 'on stage'. Some writers find it temptingly easy to consign the actual events of their plot to the text breaks or to the intervals between chapters and then have the characters *talk* about them. This is one of the reasons why plans that are full of action and movement can give rise to stories that are rather static and apt to run out of steam.

When enlivening a plot by introducing some unanticipated action you do have to beware of two contradictory dangers. On the one hand, the innovation may have consequences so extravagant or elaborate that they begin to distort or even take over the scheme of the story. On the other hand, if it is given no relevance at all within the larger scheme the innovation may seem to be entirely gratuitous. A pointless diversion may serve to get your story moving again, but is likely to leave it just as firmly stuck once the diversion is over. In deciding what you will introduce into your story, it may be best to contrive an event which results in some small but important revelation, or an event which leaves a small but unsettling legacy. For instance, an event which inflicts a minor injury on your hero may be sufficiently dramatic to get your plot moving again, and it ought to be possible to make the injury in question serve as an extra handicap to some difficult action which the hero must perform in the eventual climax.

Getting out of an inextricable plot-tangle is usually harder than injecting some movement into a becalmed story. If a character gets into a tight corner from which extraction is difficult this can usually be accomplished by introducing the required assistance. This may be done by introducing a Good Samaritan or by allowing the character to find exactly the implement he needs lurking in his pocket. In the latter case, it is always a good idea to go back to an earlier stage of the story and introduce the item in question so that it will seem to your reader to be a legitimate narrative move. I shall call this 'back-referencing'. It is the necessity of coping with difficulties of this kind which leads unscrupulous fantasy writers to use Nick Lowe's 'get-out-of-jail-free cards'.

Greater difficulties arise when your plot gets to a stage where it no longer seems to make sense. This is a common problem because it is partly psychological. Writers often start a story bursting with energy and enthusiasm, and when the initial fervour wears off the story often seems to lose its strength. Furthermore, if you are writing a long story with a complicated plot you may well reach a stage where you have no idea how much your readers will be able to perceive or deduce at a particular point in the text; because you already know what the whole scheme looks like, you cannot put yourself in the shoes of people who only know what they have so far read. If your plot comes to seem hopeless or worthless, therefore, you must first consider the possibility that the fault lies in your own eye rather than the text. Sometimes, the advice of a fresh eye can be useful – it is at this stage that writers who don't mind sharing their work-in-progress are apt to take advice from 'story doctors', always hoping to receive the news that they are worrying unnecessarily and that their brainchild is perfectly healthy.

Sometimes, alas, the fault really is in the story. Again, a fresh eye might be able to put the problem into a different perspective, but you might be faced with the awful prospect of having to loosen the knot at an earlier point in the story, by going back and taking out some of the complication which caused the entanglement. There are some problems for which the only cure is doing it again, taking a little more care. There are even some for which there is no cure at all. But you should never be in too much of a hurry to give up in disgust, because that can become such an easy way out that you find it difficult to finish anything at all. Some stories do have to be abandoned, but that should always be a last resort.

The advent of word processors has made troubleshooting much less time-consuming. They make back-referencing of plot adjustments much easier. They also make it easy for writers whose own energies are flagging to go back a few thousand words and tinker with the text as they move towards the place at which they stopped, hoping to build up sufficient momentum to carry them past the sticking-point and get the story moving again.

Doing without plots

If your story is to get by without a plot it needs some other connecting thread to link the beginning to the end. If the story is to have any aesthetic shape at all it will probably be necessary for the end to refer to the beginning, perhaps showing the opening scene or declaration in a new light. Much can sometimes be achieved with a recurrent motif of some kind: an image or a phrase which crops up at intervals within the story, its meaning subtly shifted at each invocation. Some very short stories can get away with two invocations, but three is much more effective and more than three may seem to be labouring the point.

A short piece of prose without a plot is likely to seem more like a 'prose poem' than a story, and there is a rich tradition of prose poetry in fantasy fiction, extending from Edgar Allan Poe and Charles Baudelaire through the works of various writers associated with the 'Lovecraft circle' – especially Clark Ashton Smith – to such contemporary avant-garde fantasists as Thomas Ligotti. In such works the description of a fantastic environment or a bizarre sequence of events takes precedence over the exploits of particular characters. If such stories have characters – and some do not – the character in question is likely to undergo a single revelatory experience rather than undertake an active project.

Many stories of this kind are presented as visions and it is probable that many actual dreams are transmuted into stories of this nature. It is probable that all writers of fantasy fiction take an intense interest in their own dreams, and I imagine that many must feel – as I invariably do – that many a nice dream is ruined as potential source-material by the unfortunate nonsensicality of what passes for its plot.

The importance of the visionary imagination in fantasy and science fiction encourages the production of stories whose plots are mere tokenistic devices to contain images and ideas. The longest novels, as well as the shortest stories, often dispense with all but the merest shadow of a plot and many novels present plots which are never untangled and which defy the very possibility of disentanglement. Some of the great classics of fantastic fiction are stories whose plots never come remotely close to making sense, and which become classics partly because of it as well as partly in spite of it. (Consider, for example, James Hogg's *Confessions of a Justified Sinner*, William Hope Hodgson's *The House on the Borderland* or Frank Herbert's *Dune*.) Some others are projects whose scope is so expansive as to make any thought of plotting virtually irrelevant. (Consider, for instance, Olaf Stapledon's *Last and First Men*, John Crowley's *Little, Big* or Robert Irwin's *The Arabian Nightmare*.) Some lovers of fantasy fiction consider plotting to be a vulgar matter of no real importance by comparison with visionary power – and many readers sympathise with that view, although few editors do.

It is often useful in planning even the vastest projects to have a character with a personal agenda that can somehow encompass the awesome vision and draw a personal meaning from it – like the man on the hill in Stapledon's *Star Maker* or Nigel Walmsley in Gregory Benford's novel series concluded with *Sailing Bright Eternity* – but such enterprises must work on their own terms rather than relying upon the pulling power of their plots. They must be intrinsically fascinating, and the connections which bind their parts together into a coherent whole must be thematic or allegorical rather than matters of challenge, complication and climax.

Writers who are particularly interested in the visionary aspects of their plots (as I am) may need to take a rather cavalier attitude to the business of designing plots that can contain great panoramas of space or time. It is sometimes helpful to juxtapose the intensely serious with the flamboyantly playful, as I tried to do in *The Hunger and Ecstasy of Vampires*. James Morrow describes this enthusiasm for tackling large themes as 'swatting at the cosmos' (quoting a creative writing tutor who was forever warning students against doing it) and his unrepentant verve for tackling such projects has resulted in some of the finest modern examples of comedies in deadly earnest, including *Towing Jehovah* and *Blameless in Abaddon*.

Where do you get your ideas from?

All science fiction writers are asked this question wherever they go because science fiction stories, far more than any other kind, tend to be based on new or seemingly new ideas. There is no easy answer to it, although many writers tired of being asked simply answer 'Anywhere'. What is really important is not the identification of places where you might go looking for ideas but the attitude of mind which you must adopt to any and all potential sources.

Story ideas do not exist in a pre-formed state, like fossils or diamonds which merely await excavation; they are the products of enquiring minds. A story idea comes into being when a would-be writer stumbles across an overheard statement, or a news item, or a story written by someone else, and thinks 'What if that were taken to its logical extreme?' or 'What if the real explanation were the opposite of the one being suggested?' or 'What if the device were to be used for *that* purpose instead of the one intended?' or 'What are the darker possibilities of that bright idea?' or 'What if the tables were turned and the victor became the victim?' – or any one of a hundred similar metamorphic exercises.

I get most of my story ideas from other fantasy and science fiction stories. They arise – quite naturally, it seems to me, although the 'naturalness' is presumably the result of long practice – at points in the stories where there seems to me to be an unexplored consequence of the central premise, or where it looks as if the story might be more interesting if the central premise were turned on its head. Scientific journalism is a less useful source than it may seem, although news of new scientific projects or accounts of new ethical dilemmas thrown up by emergent technologies can offer raw material for near-future stories. My second-best source is probably papers read at academic conferences, which are useful partly because even the most boring academic analyses can suggest new ways of approaching stories on the theme in question and partly because the fact that so many of them are boring creates an interval of quiet for the mind and the imagination to wander freely.

Most stories need two ideas rather than one, although many readers only notice the one which provides the story with its novum, taking for granted the one which moves the characters through their particular plot. Most ideas of the former sort could actually be deployed in lots of different stories – and many of them are – while ideas of the latter kind are usually unique to a single story.

For example, when I read in my daily newspaper that someone had proposed genetically engineering pigs so that their hearts would be suitable for humans in need of transplants it seemed to be an obvious cue for a story, but I still needed the story itself. It so happened that a few days earlier I had been watching a teen-angst chat show on TV, in which a girl whose parents were in the process of breaking up confessed that their well-intentioned attempts to involve her in their discussions were causing her some anguish. 'They keep asking me what I want,' she said, 'and I don't know!' That poignant cry provided me with a plot thread that I could use to draw the central character – the little girl in need of the heart transplant – through the plot.

It was easy enough to organise the story in question into a series of scenes in which the two parents conduct a private war by offering opposed accounts of what their daughter 'wants' and 'needs', while the daughter maintains an assiduous neutrality, trying to keep everyone happy. Looking up 'heart' in my dictionary of quotations quickly directed me to a couplet in Alexander Pope's 'Essay on Morals' which provided both a title and a name for the central character: 'What can Chloé want?' (The second half of the couplet is 'she wants a heart'; it refers, ironically, to someone who is 'heartless' in a purely metaphorical sense, but one of the small delights of writing science fiction is the ability to add irony to irony by literalising metaphors.) The story can be found in the March 1994 issue of *Asimov's Science Fiction*.

4
HAPPILY EVER AFTER: ENDINGS

Ritual endings

When they begin a story, readers usually know how it will end. In much the same way that 'Once upon a time' sets certain expectations in place when used as an opening, 'And they lived happily ever after' reassures us that what has been set to rights will stay that way.

Many genres of popular fiction have ritual endings of the 'happily ever after' kind. A genre romance usually ends with an honest declaration by the hero that he has discovered a deep and abiding love for the heroine. A murder mystery usually ends with the exposure of the murderer's identity as a result of the careful application of the detective's powers of reasoning. A Hitchcockian thriller usually ends with the hero discovering the meaning and significance of the 'McGuffin', the mysterious object which his various tempters and persecutors have been trying to obtain, and making use of this information to thwart the villains. A western usually ends with a confrontation in which the good gunslinger will outdraw and kill the evil gunslinger. Secondary-world fantasies, like Ruritanian romances, usually end with the restoration of the rightful king to his throne and the banishment of the would-be usurper or Dark Lord.

Although readers know how all these kinds of story usually end, they also know that there are exceptions. Not *all* stories of these kinds end the way they 'ought to'. Writers may ingeniously vary or cunningly pervert these outcomes in the interests of novelty, irony or tragedy. It is worth re-stating, however, that novelty can only arise against a background of the expected, and that there could not be such a thing as a sense of irony or a sense of tragedy if certain expectations were not in place to be violated. For instance, Shakespeare's tragedies would not be 'tragic' were we not to feel that Romeo and Juliet 'ought' to be allowed to marry and settle down in domestic harmony and that Othello's misunderstandings regarding Desdemona's alleged treachery 'ought' to be cleared up.

The 'expected' outcomes which stories have are not intended to be taken for granted, even by readers who would feel cheated and outraged were a detective to fail to solve the mystery confronting him or the heroine of a romance to be unceremoniously rejected by the hero. Dramatic tension requires that the realisation of the expected outcome should always seem to be in doubt. The suspensefulness of your work will depend on your cleverness in complicating your plots, thus constructing tortuous obstacle-courses which your characters must negotiate before arriving – or, sometimes, not arriving – at their apparent destination.

From the reader's viewpoint, the expected ending of a story functions rather like a 'magnetic pole' towards which the narrative's compass always points. The sense which readers have of 'knowing where they are' within a story is often dependent on knowing where they are heading, and the plot's direction towards its magnetic pole is closely connected with the precious sense of *involvement* which is one of the excitements of reading. When readers claim that they 'couldn't put a book down' they usually mean that the urgency with which they wanted to keep following the compass-heading of the plot was powerful enough to over-ride their more mundane aims and duties. If you can instil this sense of urgency in your readers they will be grateful to you.

This does not necessarily mean that you must *always* know exactly where your story is headed. There have been some very accomplished 'make it up as you go' writers and there must have been many books which ended up in a manner very different from that which the writer had in mind to start with. It does mean, though, that by the time you have finished revising your work the text must read as if it was always inevitable that it should end as it does. You will undoubtedly encounter difficulties if you try to steer your narrative without even the vaguest notion where it is going, and you may write yourself into a corner if you veer so far from your original course that you cannot recover your original heading.

Unfortunately, long stories almost invariably do veer off course at some stage and, as the preceding chapter's section on 'troubleshooting' admitted, there will be times when you have to agonise over the question of whether to steer it back again – excusing the detour on the grounds that it was the scenic route – or whether to set a new course for a different destination.

Twists in the tail

The main reason so many kinds of stories have these quasi-ritualistic outcomes is, of course, a corollary of the fact that worlds within texts possess an innate moral order. 'The good ended happily, and the bad unhappily. That is what fiction means,' as Miss Prism explained to Cecily in *The Importance of Being Earnest*. Not all the expectations relevant to story-telling are moral ones, however, and there are many stories whose basic mechanism is to establish false expectations which are then cleverly violated.

Many jokes and anecdotes function in this fashion. Although few jokes actually have plots, their form often mimics the three-step pattern of challenge, complication and climax. The first part of the story establishes a pattern, the second step extends it in one direction, and the third performs a sidestep which removes it to a different – and hopefully unexpected – conclusion.

Examples of this kind of pseudo-plot include all jokes beginning 'There was an Englishman, a Scotsman and an Irishman...' One fantasy variant has the three individuals lost in the desert when they find a lamp such as Aladdin's, whose resident genie offers them one wish each. The Englishman says: 'I'm *so* hungry; I wish I were in the Savoy Grill enjoying a nice juicy steak' – and his wish is granted. The Scotsman says: 'I'm *so* thirsty – I wish I were in my favourite pub in Glasgow enjoying a pint of beer' – and his wish is granted. The Irishman says: 'It's *so* lonely out here; I wish I had the Englishman and the Scotsman to keep me company.'

When I talk publicly in colleges or libraries about my career in science fiction I often explain that it is the result of a misspent youth; when I ought to have been out in the great wide world learning to drink, gamble and seduce women I was at home reading and writing science fiction. I always close the anecdote by reassuring the audience that I suffered no lasting harm. 'In time,' I say, 'I learned to drink – moderately. Eventually, I learned to gamble – carefully. And in the end I learned the most valuable lesson of all – to tell myself that two out of three ain't bad.'

The kinds of story associated with such masters of the surprise ending as O. Henry and Roald Dahl – in the latter's *Tales of the Unexpected* rather than his children's books – do not always use this three-step pattern, but they invariably follow a pattern which involves laying down groundwork that points in one direction and then performing a 'knight's move' which leads to an unanticipated outcome. The outcome in question is usually specified in a brief punch-line – the point of the exercise is not to enjoy the destination but merely to touch down.

Most climactic plot-twists are intended to take the reader by surprise, and will usually be counted as failures if they do not. However, jokes which elicit a tired groan rather than a laugh are sometimes intended to do exactly that – as 'shaggy dog stories' and 'sick jokes' usually are. Stories which belong to the genre which the French call *contes cruels* – whose punch-lines are intended to horrify rather than to amuse – may offer revelations which merely confirm, in some deftly nasty-minded fashion, what the reader has been expecting all along.

An element of revelation is, of course, compulsory in mystery stories. Although the end of the story is ritualised, in that the protagonist must discover the identity of the murderer and deliver him to justice, the details of the discovery ought to come as a surprise. Ideally, the revelation ought to lie on the very edge of expectability; the reader will be disappointed if the answer was too easily anticipated, and just as disappointed if there was no way at all that the solution could be deduced from the clues offered in the course of the story.

Producing acceptable twists in the tails of your stories is a vexing business because it is never easy to calculate where the edge of expectability lies, and readers differ markedly in their ability to stay in step with the writer. It is probably inevitable that a story of this kind which is greeted with delight in some quarters will fall flat in others, just as the joke which prompts gales of laughter in the company to which it is new may be rudely dismissed by an audience who have already heard it.

Inexperienced writers often get frustrated because editors and readers do not seem to appreciate the cleverness of their concluding twists – usually because they have seen their like a hundred times before. Like beauty, alas, cleverness is in the eye of the beholder. Many inexperienced writers get so hung up on the quest for twists in the tail that will work that they sometimes forget that the vast majority of stories do not have such twists at all, and most of those that do also have a good deal of story value in addition to their final twists.

There is a curious paradox involved in writing 'tales of the unexpected' for readers who know that the story they are reading belongs to that category. If such readers are presented with a scenario in which character A has recruited character B to assist in a plot to deceive character C, it ought to be obvious that in order to qualify as a tale of the unexpected what must *really* be happening is that character C is secretly in league with character A (or possibly B) and that the ultimate loser will be B (or possibly A). The fact that alert readers will always be able to penetrate the first layer of deception forces cleverer writers to employ 'double switch' endings in which stripping away the first layer of pretence is only a prelude to the climactic removal of a second layer. Such recomplications are particularly popular in the theatre, often featuring in plays which have one-word titles (e.g. *Sleuth*, *Deadfall* and *Corpse*). Writers possessed of unusual ingenuity occasionally contrive triple-switch endings, but if you do that you will run the risk of leaving your audience in a state of utter confusion

Science fiction is particularly conducive to the construction of twist in the tail endings because so many stories in the genre involve trying to work out the logical consequences of a novel idea. Given that you can take as much time as you like in planing your story and working out the possibilities inherent in your story's novum, whereas your readers only have the time it takes them to read the story, it ought to be possible for you to find a few possibilities which, although perfectly logical, will not be immediately obvious to your readers. On the other hand, one of the difficulties faced by novice writers is that many of their readers will have read a good deal more science fiction than they have, and may well have had abundant opportunity to study the realm of possibilities that the novice is entering for the first time.

One of the most popular sub-genres of science fiction is the time paradox story, which examines possible ways of working out what might happen if, for instance, a time-traveller were to shoot one of his own ancestors before the ancestor in question had a chance to procreate. Unfortunately, so many twists in this kind of story have already been explored that the task of finding a new one has become very daunting.

If you want to write a story of this kind you are faced with a choice between assiduously researching what has been done and trying to work out a new device or trying to direct your story towards an audience which is just as naive as you are. Either way, every broadcast episode of *Red Dwarf* is likely to put another nail into the coffin of your hopes – but on the brighter side, every twist you discover and study might trigger the idea for a slight variation which would be just novel enough, and just tricky enough, to please even the most jaded connoisseur of the species.

Normalising endings

Even the kinds of stories which belong to popular genres are sufficiently diverse to make any simple classification of their endings problematic, but the various ritual endings appropriate to particular genres can be sorted out into two broad categories.

The first such category consists of all the ritual endings whose effect is simply to restore a 'normality' which has somehow been disrupted. In detective stories and thrillers crime is seen as an unfortunate interruption of the course of everyday affairs: a break which demands repair. (Crime is, of course, classified by sociologists as 'deviance'.) In supernatural horror stories, the disruption of our world by malevolent visitations is a violation of the natural order which similarly requires healing by some kind of narrative exorcism. In the endings of stories of these kinds, the favoured characters are saved from the threats which hang over them (or not, in tragic variants) and enabled to resume the course of their normal lives.

The restored normalities of much popular fiction are not, of course, free from further violation – which is good news for writers contemplating sequels. A detective's triumph over a particular murderer cannot put an end to murder, and if he proves popular he can be confronted with an infinite series of breaches to heal. For this reason, some writers have been able to build entire careers on the exploits of a single detective – and detective stories are readily adaptable to the TV medium, where the rigours of weekly scheduling put a high priority on the series format. By contrast, the heroine of a romance can hardly repeat her success over and over again – true love (where true means 'faithful' rather than 'authentic') is supposed to last forever. Writers of romantic fiction tend, therefore, to slot different characters into the same formula, and TV schedules have great difficulty in accommodating romances.

This difference helps to explain the different characteristic formats of various sub-genres of science fiction and fantasy and the differences in their adaptability to other media. Mystery stories with normalising endings are relatively easy to shift into science fiction, where future agencies of law enforcement can not only solve crimes but unravel problems whose solution relies on the expectable but as-yet-unexpected logical consequences of the central story idea. *Star Trek* and *The X-Files* both employ this kind of format; the exploratory thrust of the science-fictional mythology of the conquest of space allows the *Star Trek* characters to move on from one problematic situation to another – boldly going, as the introduction has it, where no one has gone before.

Normalising endings were, for a while, almost compulsory when writing fantasy because it came to be seen as necessary to 'excuse' the fantastic content of a story by writing it off as a dream. The ultimate normalising ending is '...and then I woke up'. This is, however, such a blatant cheat that it was run into the ground a hundred years ago and is now considered to be beneath contempt.

Normalising endings of the kinds used in other genres are not so easily imported into modern fantasy. Attempts to adapt fantasy to the series format favoured by TV have been forced to institute such strange sub-genres as the 'vampire cop' story and the 'wandering angel' story – both of which are way out on the fringes of the text-based genre. The 'wandering barbarian' sub-genre of heroic fantasy is the only one which can readily sustain an infinite series involving a single protagonist (Robert E. Howard's Conan series, subsequently carried forward by many other hands, is the most obvious example), although comic fantasies set in a single absurd milieu but not necessarily using the same characters have recently enjoyed huge success under the guidance of Terry Pratchett and Piers Anthony. Other fantasy series tend to be strictly limited in scope, more like serials than series – which is why they very often come in packages of three or six.

If you are interested in writing science fiction you might well be attracted to the kinds of science fiction which use normalising endings. They are easier to imagine and design than other kinds of endings because all that you have to do is restore the same conditions that you established in the beginning. You also have the possibility of getting further mileage out of the work you put into the construction of your imaginary world – furthermore, these worlds can be further elaborated in each story you add to the series, eventually building up a wealth of detail that no single story could sensibly contain. There is, however, an important sense in which normalising endings are somewhat ill-fitted to the science fiction genre.

Normalising endings in science fiction

The problem with normalising endings is that they take for granted that normality is a goal worth aiming for and that any disruption of the status quo is bad. A science fiction story about a new invention which aims towards a normalising ending must take it for granted that the invention has to be eradicated. This is absurd, on two counts. Firstly, it is patently obvious that many new inventions are actually beneficial – and genre science fiction has always based its claim to intellectual seriousness on its recognition of the great importance of technological progress. Secondly, it is extremely difficult to 'unmake' a discovery once it has been made; even if the inventor is blown up along with his machine (as usually happens in this kind of normalising science fiction story) the fact that the technical possibility has been established means that the invention can always be made again, and again.

This problem is so acute that Isaac Asimov coined the term 'Frankenstein syndrome' to refer to stories in which new machines run amok, destroy their creators and have to be destroyed in their turn. He pointed out that this kind of story is tacitly technophobic, and that the continual production of such works offers a tacit allegorical account of mankind's relationship to technology which is the opposite of the true one – that we owe everything we possess, including our notion of 'human nature', to the products of technology.

This does not mean, of course, that science fiction stories with normalising endings do not work *as stories*. From *Frankenstein* itself to *Jurassic Park,* the genre has been dominated by such stories, which have always retained the power to thrill their readers. In the meantime, though – and Asimov thought that the two phenomena were connected – the rapid acceleration of technological progress in the last two centuries has been accompanied by a dramatic increase in technophobia.

This difficulty is not so pronounced in stories set in a moderately distant future, partly because the 'normality' which is being restored can be defined in terms of a new phase of technological advancement. It ought to be noted, however, that stories of this type tend to rely heavily on disruptions involving alien beings – as, of course, do contemporary invasion stories of the *War of the Worlds* variety. Again, if such stories are to use normalising endings they must take it for granted that all aliens are nasty and must be eradicated. Such stories can – and often do – avoid implicit technophobia by making a new invention the means of destroying the alien, but the cost of that move is to embrace a tacit xenophobia which might be deemed equally undesirable.

An ingenious variant of the alien menace story which has become very popular in recent years is the 'secret invasion' formula in which constant disruptions of normality can be attributed to a single source which remains permanently hidden; its individual manifestations can therefore be countered while leaving open the possibility for endless repetition. This kind of story is tailor-made for TV because it combines series potential with everyday settings (thus cutting costs) but anyone familiar with such TV manifestations as *The Invaders* and *Dark Skies* will appreciate that its indefinite extension serves to build a very powerful sense of paranoia whose focus inevitably spreads from the aliens themselves to infect individual humans and human institutions.

Stories of this kind do work very well, as melodramas – but you might want to ask yourself, before making such stories the mainstay of your career, what kind of moral order you would like to support and sustain. Worlds within texts cannot avoid moral order, so neutrality is not an option.

Wish-fulfilment endings

The second broad category of ritual endings consists, of course, of all those in which the situation of the favoured characters is significantly improved. Sometimes this improvement is represented as a fairly commonplace achievement – the success in love achieved by the heroines of genre romance is often viewed as a kind of natural entitlement – but it is usually more lavish. Tales of financial enrichment rarely deal in sums as trifling as the average industrial wage; proverbial wisdom may speak of 'wealth beyond the dreams of avarice' but popular fiction suggests that there is no such thing. In real life, hardly anyone ever lives 'happily ever after', but such is the creative power of writers that readers of fiction are often unprepared to settle for anything less.

Wish-fulfilment endings feature prominently in the stories we constantly make up about ourselves for private consumption, which we usually call daydreams. People rarely talk about their daydreams – perhaps their most private and most intimate possessions – but we can be fairly certain that most daydreamers rarely bother fantasising about little rewards and petty triumphs; while it's all in the mind you might as well go the whole hog.

It is probable that the main reason why people rarely talk about their daydreams is the embarrassment of their utter lack of realism and abundant generosity. Were we to repeat our private fantasies aloud they would inevitably be misconstrued as actual ambitions, or at least as hopes, and would then seem absurd; we are, alas, all too well aware of the vanity of human wishes. In fact, we usually use such fantasies as consolations – meagre but nevertheless precious compensations for our actual trials and tribulations.

Public wish-fulfilment fantasies tend to be more modest than private ones, even though the power which narrators have to manufacture rewards is unrestricted by the limits of possibility or probability. Writers can and do work miracles of reckless generosity, but even the wildest fantasist must pay some heed to the bounds of the reasonable in order to conserve plausibility. It is worth noting, however, that the first man ever to make a million dollars from his writing was Edgar Rice Burroughs, whose work may have come closer to the texture, substance and sheer exuberance of daydreams than anyone had done before. James Thurber's account of *The Secret Life of Walter Mitty* is a fine comedy, but it is probable that no one who ever laughed at poor Walter did so without a slight twinge of guilt.

Given that we all use our ability to fantasise in the production of wish-fulfilment dreams, it is hardly surprising that there are whole genres of popular fiction devoted to similar ends. Nor is it surprising, however, that the genre which thrives most extravagantly is the one which celebrates the only kind of triumph that could – conceivably, at least – be available to everyone without some radical disruption of the world as we know it. Becoming rich, famous or a world champion sportsperson can only be the privilege of the few, but everybody might find true love if – as is sometimes alleged – our idiosyncrasies were so organised that everyone had a different perfect partner.

There are, of course, a great many stories set in the known world in which the central characters do become successful in every kind of competition, acquiring wealth, status, celebrity *and* true love. There are many readers, however, who find it slightly discomfiting to juxtapose such fantasies of known-world success with the ordinariness of their actual lives. Identifying with the characters in such stories is exhilarating, but the more extravagant the ending of the story, the more it will contrast with the real circumstances to which the reader must return – and some readers find that jarring and saddening.

Because the worlds they contain are so determinedly unrealistic, secondary-world fantasies are insulated from this kind of collision with actuality and the distress that might accompany it. The fantasy world is, by definition, unreal, so stepping back into reality involves no discomfort. The successes which characters obtain in fantastic worlds are entirely distinct from the competitions of everyday life, and they can be enjoyed by the reader *to the full*.

Even the most extravagant fantasy which adopts the known world as its stage cannot do more for its readers than enable them to identify with a fabulously rich film star who also happens to be an aristocrat, a sporting champion, a world-class sexual athlete and a diehard enemy of the Mafia – and even that may seem a little over the top. A secondary-world fantasy can offer the opportunity to become the universally acknowledged and universally beloved High King of Everywhere, or the noble champion who will secure his throne. In the course of obtaining that goal, the king or champion will, of course, defeat a Dark Lord who is not merely villainous but the very personi-fication and embodiment of evil. Most fantasies are, in fact, more modest than that – but even the modest ones can play in a blithely casual manner with powers and opportunities that make *all* mundane wish-fulfilments (except perhaps for true love) seem relatively worth-less.

The main difficulty facing writers of known-world wish-fulfilment fantasies is the construction of a plausible route to the peak of achievement. By contrast, the main difficulty facing writers of secondary-world wish-fulfilment fantasies is to make the route to the peak seem far more difficult than it actually is. In an arena where magic always provides a means of making anything happen without the necessity of a chain of causes and effects, happy endings are very easily contrived – and they can be contrived *instantly*, no matter how desperate the situation of the characters might be.

The earliest Greek dramas followed a standard pattern in which the human characters would get themselves into inextricable difficulties, which would then be sorted out by a god. To signify that the god was descending from Olympus, the actor playing him would be lowered on to the stage by a device of ropes and pulleys: the first of all theatrical 'special effects'. He thus became, in Greek, a *deus ex machina* – a god from the machine. In the critical jargon, *deus ex machina* now refers to any contrivance which sorts out a tangled plot by arbitrary intervention.

Ending your stories by *deus ex machina* is likely to be seen by sensitive readers as a form of cheating. In any fantastic fiction, however, *deus ex machina* endings are always available, and it could be argued that they cannot really be avoided. In a science fiction story the characters can always come up with exactly the invention required to solve the problem with which they are faced, and in a fantasy story they only have to discover the right magic spell. The artistry of fantasy writing is largely a matter of making it appear that you cannot and will not invoke a *deus ex machina* ending, even though that is exactly what you intend to do – for the very good reason that in most kinds of fantasy and science fiction there is nothing else you can do to resolve your climaxes.

At the end of a wish-fulfilment fantasy you will require a settlement that could not possibly be attained by any means other than magic, but you must try as hard as you possibly can to pretend that you are not simply 'waving a magic wand'. You must do your utmost to make the ultimate victory seem both hard-won and legitimately won.

Given that the practicality of the final victory in a wish-fulfilment fantasy is arbitrary, requiring only that a set of magical conditions you have invented is fully met, it is usually as well to deflect your reader's attention to the story's moral propriety. If you are writing wish-fulfilment fantasy you will find it useful to devise exceedingly nasty villains, but you will also find it useful not to oppose them with exceedingly pious heroes. The best strategy is to employ hesitant and fallible heroes who must learn – slowly and painfully – how to attain the heroic state of mind necessary for their ultimate success. They must eventually become *worthy* to precipitate the final *deus ex machina*, and you would be wise to make that attainment a lengthy and carefully measured process.

This necessity can, of course, become a virtue. It tends to have the effect of making all wish-fulfilment fantasies into parables of personal maturation. This makes them especially attractive to teenagers, who can hardly help being acutely aware of all the difficulties involved in the frustratingly slow progress from childhood to adulthood. The best wish-fulfilment fantasies are those which offer the most sensitive alle-gorical analyses of the teenage predicament and the most heartening moral support. The fact that many critics consider wish-fulfilment fantasies to be 'children's books' ought to be considered a compliment rather than an insult. The fact that adults can still read such books with great pleasure is *not* evidence of such readers' continuing imma-turity, but evidence of the fact that the process of becoming a fully aware and morally competent human being requires a whole lifetime, and then some.

Improving endings in science fiction

It might appear at first glance that using improving endings gets around the difficulties which make normalising endings inappropriate to science fiction stories whose writers are anxious to avoid techno-phobia and xenophobia. They allow the inventor's new machine to be counted a blessing rather than a curse and the celebration of the spacefarer's landing to be assessed as 'a giant leap for mankind'.

So useful is this kind of forward-looking ending that writers who want to exploit the melodramatic potential of machines run amok, alien invasions and terrible natural disasters often try to cheer up normal-ising endings by asserting that mankind has learned a valuable lesson which is bound to work to the future benefit of society. A striking example of this kind of narrative move can be found at the end of Arthur Conan Doyle's novella *The Poison Belt*.

The principal problem which besets the use of improving endings in science fiction is that you have to decide what will actually count as an improvement. The problem with the improvements that can be taken for granted in known-world fiction – wealth, fame, status, and so on – is that they are not automatically transferable to a future setting. We understand exactly what such things signify in our world, but they are bound to seem less *relevant* in science-fictional settings. There is a sense in which *all* known-world stories are about wealth, fame, status and so on – or about the lack of them – but science fiction stories are, by definition, usually focused on other matters. Even true love, although it holds its narrative value better than its rivals, is less significant in science fiction than in fiction which is entirely bounded by known-world concerns.

The reduced relevance of wealth, fame and status in science fiction means that science fiction stories often focus on the one kind of success that *is* always and unambiguously relevant: the valuable lesson. The uplift which science fiction writers tend to find most convenient as a narrative north pole is a climactic enlightenment. This often involves an actual displacement of some kind, because it is a good idea to symbolise enlightenment with some kind of supportive image – for example, the spaceship lifting off for the unknown, or finally making its hard-won landfall – but the essence of such endings is the main character's attainment of a better state of mind. This is sometimes referred to in the critical jargon as a 'conceptual breakthrough'.

It is probably true to say that figuring out how best to end a science fiction story is more difficult than figuring out how to end any other kind of story. You can, of course, avoid the question of what would count as a viable improving ending by ducking it entirely and opting for a twist in the tail ending or a *conte cruel* ending which will deliver a relatively unsympathetic character to an ironically appropriate fate. If such stories are to be more than mere jokes, however, they do need to pay some attention to the longer view opened up by the possibilities inherent in the story's central idea. A writer who refuses to acknowledge the possibility of conceptual breakthrough risks being seen as a coward or a clown, if not a mere fool.

It is not easy for science fiction stories to deliver any authentic enlightenment to their readers. We cannot know today that which will not be discovered until tomorrow, so the best that even the cleverest science fiction writer can hope to contrive is to point out as-yet-unrealised consequences of what we already know. Expressions of enthusiasm by science fiction readers, however, have always tended to focus on an exciting and liberating *impression* of enlightenment gained from a particular story – an experience awakening a new appreciation of the actual magnitude of the universe revealed by modern science. Such experiences can be sufficiently powerful to precipitate a quasi-religious conversion. The chances are that if you want to be a science fiction writer you are already a science fiction reader and that you have already undergone some rite of passage of this sort.

You do not actually have to become a competent philosopher before you can write science fiction, but if you want to write good science fiction you will have to cultivate a philosophical attitude. The kind of enlightenment which most of your readers will be looking for is usually called a 'sense of wonder', although modern readers sometimes become embarrassed by the implication of wide-eyed naivety that the term carries and like to emphasise their supposed sophistication by using the derisory spelling 'sensawunda'. Cultivating a philosophical attitude does not require you to perform grandiose feats of invention, but it does require you to look at all possibilities, and all actualities, with the aid of a cosmic perspective. William Blake summed it up rather well in 'Auguries of Innocence' when he recommended that we should attempt:

> To see a world in a grain of sand
> And a heaven in a wild flower
> Hold infinity in the palm of your hand
> And eternity in an hour.

However trivial the events in a science fiction story are, the world within the text is still a world: a world with a future as well as a present, where the stars beckon even if they are not attainable. If you want to contrive appropriate endings for your science fiction stories you have to bear that in mind, and if you do so sensitively enough it will probably steer you towards apt conclusions. An editor raised in the old school of story design once complained of one of one of my stories – the first one he had seen – that 'it gets kinda preachy at the end'. Actually, they all do and they always will, and I am not about to start apologising for it.

Upbeat and downbeat endings

Most readers prefer to read stories with happy endings most of the time. Because they know this, most editors like to publish a majority of stories with happy endings. On the other hand, most literary critics consider stories with happy endings to be unrealistic and artificial, and thus intrinsically less *worthy* than stories which employ tragic and ironic variations.

Writers often feel that this difference of opinion catches them between a rock and a hard place. It often seems that if they give the editors and readers what they want the critics might end up despising them, whereas if they aim for critical approval they will never reach a large enough audience to make a living. It is possible to have it both ways – critical approval can go hand in hand with commercial success and sometimes offers a significant boost in that direction – but combining the two objectives often seems to the inexperienced writer rather like walking a narrow and fraying tightrope.

It is probable that fear of critical disapproval is not the most signifi- cant factor that inclines writers to be much less fond of happy endings than readers or editors. Writing is a form of self-expression and many people simply do not feel particularly upbeat about themselves, their lives or the world. The popular notion that all writers are angst-ridden misfits is a myth, but writing is a solitary occupation and it requires a certain degree of introspection and self-discipline. Those writers who are exuberant pleasure-seekers by inclination and the life and soul of every party have no option but to change down through their mental gears when they sit down to work. However, the simple fact is that writers are, on the whole, somewhat less enthusiastic to write upbeat stories than editors are to publish them.

I have known more than one editor whose advice to authors with downbeat tendencies was always brutally forthright: 'You have to decide whether you're working for the punters or posterity, and if it's for posterity, don't expect the punters to pay for it.' This is, of course, an over-simplification. No one who ever set pen to paper really wrote exclusively for 'the punters' or exclusively for 'posterity'. Everyone who wants to be taken seriously also wants to be read, and everyone who wants to be read also wants to be taken seriously. Nor is any audi- ence as relentlessly crude in its tastes or as firmly set in its ways as to warrant dismissive summation as 'the punters'.

You do *not* have to decide whether to work for the punters or posterity, and I am not sure that there is any merit at all in thinking in those terms. It *is* as well to remember, though, that you will win the undying gratitude of the majority of your readers and avoid the derision of the most rigorous critics if you can contrive an upbeat ending that *works*. An upbeat ending which merely 'punches the right buttons' by handing out *deus ex machina* rewards to the good while visiting a hail of bullets upon the bad is always likely to be better received than an ending which refuses to do so out of mere cussedness, but you have to do more than that to hit any kind of jackpot.

Happy endings always seem less artificial if they are slightly qualified. Your upbeat conclusion will seem less formulaic – and hence more personal as well as more profound – if you take care to stress that it has not been won without cost, and might still be infected by some fatal flaw. It is nowadays conventional for horror stories to confuse their normalising endings by adding a brief coda to inform the reader that the evil has not been put away forever and that one would be deluded to imagine that it ever could be. This device is often used crudely – especially in films – but its subtler variants can import a useful note of 'realism' into the happiest ending. The only endings to which some such note of modification is inappropriate are the endings attached to the most extreme and wholehearted wish-fulfilment fantasies – that is, love stories and extravagant secondary-world fantasies. (This helps to explain why successful fantasy writers planning sequels to their first trilogies usually go back in time rather than forwards, so that the pristine perfection of their Final Battle does not need to be compromised or undone.)

By the same token, much can be done to ameliorate or excuse a downbeat ending if the awfulness of the tragedy is balanced by a small measure of moral profit. It has been argued that *Romeo and Juliet* ought not to be considered a downbeat story at all, because the tragedy of the young lovers becomes the means of healing the breach between the Montagues and the Capulets, putting a permanent end to decades of strife. One would be hard pressed to identify similar bright notes in *Othello* or *King Lear* but in both cases the damnation of the characters reveals the magnitude of their errors; the hope is that by contemplating their fates the audience might come to a better understanding of the manifestations of affection and the dangers of jealousy. It is no coincidence that tragedy is far more common in the theatre, where audience and actors occupy the same actual space, than it is in the cinema, where actors and audience are so remote from one another as almost to occupy two distinct and different worlds.

Although some editors would not agree with me, I believe that the best way to end a story is to extrapolate the sequence of events to its most fitting conclusion, and then to pay careful attention to both its upbeat *and* its downbeat qualities. If you want to insult the intelligence of your readers it is better to do it with a carrot than a stick, but it is best not to do it at all.

Some further examples

It is more difficult to provide useful examples of endings than useful examples of beginnings. A beginning and an ending both need to be understood in the context of the remainder of the story, but a beginning is the part of the story you encounter first and is thus more easily approached than the part you encounter last. Nevertheless, there may be some profit to be gained by offering two substantial examples.

This is the ending of a science-fictional comedy called 'A Career in Sexual Chemistry', which can be found in my collection *Sexual Chemistry: Sardonic Tales of the Genetic Revolution*. The story features a young man named Casanova, who becomes the butt of many jokes because of his extreme unattractiveness to girls and therefore embarks upon a career developing commercial aphrodisiacs.

In this way, Giovanni Casanova succeeded at last in adapting to his name. He lived up to the reputation of his august namesake for a year or two, and then decided that the attractions of the lifestyle were overrated. He gladdened his mother's heart by marrying again, and this time he chose a woman who was very like the earliest memories which he had of his mother. His new bride was named Janine. She had been born in Manchester, and she was embarked on a career in cosmetic cytogenics (which was the nearest thing to hairdressing that the world of 2036 could offer). She was much younger than Giovanni, but did not mind the age difference in the least.

> Giovanni and Janine favoured one another constantly with the most delicate psychochemical strokings, and learned to play the most beautiful duets with all the ingenious hormonal instruments of Giovanni's invention. But they also had a special feeling for one another – and eventually for their children – which went beyond mere chemistry and physiology: an affection which was entirely a triumph of the will. This was a treasure which, they both believed, could never have come out of one of Giovanni's test tubes.
>
> With all these advantages, they were able to live happily ever after.
>
> And so was everybody else.

Although this story is deeply steeped in sarcasm, I am particularly fond of its last line, which seemed to me to be an amplification of the traditional formula very well-suited to science fiction.

This is the ending of an equally sarcastic fantasy called 'The Phantom of Yremy', which appeared under the pseudonym Brian Craig in an anthology edited by David Pringle called *Wolf Riders*. The story tells of a judge named M. Voltigeur, famous for devising harsh punishments to fit sometimes-trivial crimes, who is plagued by a mysterious persecutor. This 'phantom' turns out to be his long-time clerk and confidant, Jean Malchance, who has reasons for hating Voltigeur that the judge is too insensitive to understand. Malchance adds insult to injury by persuading the experts who have been called in to assist the judge that the unlucky Voltigeur has himself done all the things he accuses the phantom of doing.

> Malchance was quite correct in his estimation that the people of Yremy would believe what he told them, and he had more than enough apparent proofs to convince them. He pretended to be so stricken by grief that he never served again as a clerk to the court of Yremy, but retired to live in solitude, alone with his memories and his secrets.

M. Voltigeur, who was famous while he lived as the Great Judge, became more famous still after his death, albeit briefly, as the Phantom who had haunted himself. It was said of him by many that he had devised the most fiendish of all his punishments for himself.

Whether Jean Malchance was damned for those petty magics which he had used to secure, as he saw it, a penalty uniquely fitted to his enemy's trespasses, no one knows. All that is certain is that he died but a few years after, and that just before he died he made a full confession of the whole affair – not to any eager priest of Verena or Morr, but to a wandering story-teller like myself, whom he first forced to swear that the tale should never be told within the walls of Yremy.

The inevitable result of that injunction, of course, was that everyone within those walls had heard the whole of it within a fortnight – and the lowest of the low were for once united with the highest of the high in thinking it the finest tale to which their humble town had ever given birth.

I am particularly fond of this ending because it not only provides a particularly apt confirmation of moral order but adds what seems to me to be a perceptive observation about the role which story-tellers (as opposed to judges) play in the maintenance of that order.

5

A FUNNY THING HAPPENED TO ME: VIEWPOINTS AND CHARACTERS

Narrators

There was a time when all stories were told rather than written and heard rather than read, passed on by raconteurs in an infinite series of conversations. Even now, there are many kinds of stories which still circulate in this way, including jokes and 'urban legends'. If they reach print at all they usually do so belatedly and as 'specimens' rather than works in their own right.

Usually, raconteurs place themselves as the protagonists of their story, thus establishing the 'truth' of the stories by claiming them as actual experiences. When we listen to such stories, however, we know that we need not take such claims altogether seriously, recognising that people often tell 'tall stories'. Travellers' tales need to be treated with particular scepticism, because distant locations offer wide open spaces for narrative embroidery. Such doubts about accuracy, however, do not make the stories any less compelling or any less interesting while they are being told.

When music hall comedians used to open their acts with the formula 'A funny thing happened to me on the way to the theatre tonight...', nobody actually believed that the funny thing really did happen when the comedian was on his way to the theatre. The purpose of such formulas is to establish a certain narrative *authority*, staking a claim on the hearer's willingness to believe. Such authority is powerful, as anyone knows who has ever listened raptly to a storyteller spinning out a yarn which becomes more and more preposterous by degrees, perhaps extending to the point where the raconteur deliberately breaks the spell by concluding: '...and then they killed me.'

Even when raconteurs do not stand in as their own protagonists they usually make ritual claims of authority. Urban legends are usually passed on as events which happened to 'a friend of a friend', and such claims can be taken so seriously that it becomes very hard to persuade recent hearers of a particularly juicy tale that it has actually been circulating for years and is known all over the English-speaking world. Traditional folktales often claim the alternative authority of antiquity, representing themselves as tales handed down from generation to generation since time immemorial, but that authority can be faked too, as evidenced by the fact that the Grimm brothers' collection of traditional German folktales includes one that had actually been composed only a few years earlier by Hans Christian Andersen.

Raconteurs cannot eliminate their own voices from the stories they tell. They may claim to be merely reproducing stories told to them, describing events which happened to characters who lived 'once upon a time', but their tones of voice continually shift from the insistent to the reflective. They express wonder, scepticism, confidentiality and earnest concern. They may raise questions on behalf of the audience, replying explicitly to some and swearing that their answers are true, but confessing ignorance of other matters and affecting to doubt some of the information they pass on.

Writers can, and sometimes do, attempt to make the same claims of narrative authority as raconteurs, and to play all the tricks that raconteurs do. They may write in the first person, as if their protagonists were speaking in their own voices, or they may pose as diarists recording the exploits of their friends and relatives. Even when they do this, however, they still fall prey to the essential *artifice* of writing.

Readers know that when a story is written in the first person it is a *character* who 'speaks', not the writer; on the rare occasions when writers of fiction name their protagonists after themselves – as J. G. Ballard sometimes does – the reader's response is likely to be far more wary than the response of a hearer listening to an anecdote, and this wariness cannot be dispelled by the suspicion or conviction that the story really is 'autobiographical'. The distance between writer and reader is much greater than that between raconteur and hearer, and this gives writing – even at its most intensely personal – an *objectivity* that oral discourse does not possess.

This is important to you, as a writer, for several reasons. You must, for instance, beware of assuming that exciting things which really happened will be just as exciting if you import them into a story or try to make a story out of them. The anecdote which delighted its hearers when told aloud may well seem flat and preposterous on the printed page. The narrative voice of your story is not gifted with the same kind of authority that the teller of tall tales has, so gripping readers is more complicated and more difficult than gripping listeners. On the other hand, the objectivity that writing possesses opens up opportunities that are not available to raconteurs, and the difficulties you may face in gripping your readers are amply compensated by the fact that if you *can* grip them, you can grip them harder and more securely.

Viewpoints

Because the earliest written stories were transcriptions of traditional oral tales, they usually employed 'omniscient narrators': narrators who could inform the reader about the motives, thoughts and feelings of all the characters. The objectivity of text gradually diminished the role played by 'actual' narrators who might address their audience as 'Dear reader' and often put their judgments on the events of the story into the form of a commentary, but the initial residue of this inheritance was an 'omniscient viewpoint'. Although the narrator of the story ceased to be visible within the text as an active personality, the text was still free to inform the reader about the motives, thoughts and feelings of all the characters as and when required.

Some writers still use an omniscient viewpoint but it has become very unfashionable; the vast majority of modern editors believe that what works best in print is a narrative which, although told in the third person, is tied to one particular viewpoint. If a story requires multiple viewpoints, most editors will insist that each individual section of the story is told from a single character's point of view, and that a change of viewpoint must always be preceded by a text break.

It is very common for inexperienced writers to switch viewpoints without paying any heed to this kind of textual etiquette, and almost as common for them to protest when told that it is bad practice. The fact that most editors don't like it is probably enough in itself to establish that it is best avoided, but there is a good reason for this preference.

It is possible for the reader of a text to 'enter' it and become involved with it in a way that no hearer of an oral tale ever could. Raconteurs and their hearers are always in a social situation, subject to the etiquette of conversation (and it is this etiquette which establishes the authority which requires the hearers to believe what they are told). A reader, by contrast, is alone. Even if others are present, the reader is isolated from their company because the act of reading requires that the sense of sight is disengaged from its normal function and changed into a 'translation device'. Readers cannot pay attention to others who may be present; reading texts abstracts readers from the world of 'normal' experience and removes them into a world of 'pure information'.

It is much easier for readers to enter such a world and operate within it if they can step into the shoes of a character who belongs there, seeing as that character sees and sharing the thoughts and feelings of that character. If a story requires more than one viewpoint it is very helpful to the reader if the text includes explicit signals telling the reader when to disengage from identification with one character and engage with a different one instead.

As the writer of the story you are, of course, omniscient; you know what all the characters are doing and thinking. The omniscient viewpoint will seem perfectly natural to you, and you may therefore fall into it unthinkingly, but it is wise to remember that your readers are *not* omniscient. Your readers will find it a lot easier to step into your story if you make some effort to create a suitable space, or a neatly demarcated series of suitable spaces.

Although this argument applies to all kinds of fiction it is particularly relevant to fantasy and science fiction, whose viewpoints frequently look out upon strange and exotic worlds within texts. Indeed, viewpoints in fantasy and science fiction are sometimes strange and exotic in themselves.

If your story deals with large-scale events of a kind no human viewpoint can encapsulate, then it may be necessary to adopt some kind of quasi-omniscient viewpoint, like that of a visionary or a historian, but you would still be wise to give careful consideration to the way in which your readers will enter the story and orientate themselves within it. If you insist on placing readers in the position of hearers forced to listen to a narrative voice, you will find it harder to engage their interest. In effect, you run the risk of making your story seem like a lecture, without being able to draw upon the advantages of conversational etiquette which real lecturers can learn to exploit.

Even if your story deals only with events on a scale that can conveniently be witnessed by a human observer, managing your viewpoint characters might involve far more narrative labour than managing viewpoint characters who operate in known-world situations already familiar to the reader. In fantasy and science fiction stories it is often useful to give your readers extra help to get a proper sense of their surroundings. You can do this by offering them characters for identification who will not merely observe what goes on around them but think about it and react to it. If the thoughts and the reactions are as unfamiliar as the observations, though, you might have to work hard to make sure that your readers get a series of pictures which is as clear and distinct as you can contrive.

First-person narrators

If your story has only one viewpoint character you have the option of using first-person narrative instead of third-person narrative, letting the character tell the story. This has certain advantages, although these do not include the restoration of the conversational authority that raconteurs exploit.

Some writers believe that putting their readers into the shoes of a first-person narrator creates a greater feeling of intimacy. There is probably some truth in this. Others, by contrast, think that if readers are put in the position of a first-person narrator whose attitudes are very different from their own the resultant 'discord' is greater than would be generated by a third-person narrative. There is probably some truth in this, too. There is a disarming frankness and confidentiality in the opening passages of such novels as Mary Shelley's *The Last Man* ('I am the native of a sea-surrounded nook, a cloud-enshadowed land, which, when the surface of the globe, with its shoreless ocean and trackless continents, presents itself to my mind, appears only as an inconsiderable speck of the immense whole...') but it becomes harder and harder for modern readers to identify with their antique manner of expression as time goes by.

One definite advantage of the use of first-person narrative is that it makes it easier for the writer to control the flow of the narrative. If there is a gap in the action it seems more natural for a first-person narrator to fill that gap by summing up his feelings and responses to recent events, or by indulging in some flight of fancy or speculation which will help lay the groundwork for future events, than it is to provide a third-person description of a character's reflections and anticipations.

Another advantage is that first-person narrative is generally more relaxed, by virtue of having a more conversational tone. A conversational tone does not confer any particular authority on a printed text but it does benefit from its adoption of the comfortable mannerisms of real conversation. A first-person narrative can be far less *formal* than a third-person narrative; it can make freer and more elaborate use of slang, jargon and other offbeat expressions.

The main reason some writers prefer first-person narrative is their desire to exploit this informality. It is much easier to develop a distinctive narrative voice by calculated informality than by calculated formality – which is why the styles of first-person writers such as Damon Runyon and P. G. Wodehouse are so highly individual. Informality can, moreover, be easily extended into unreliability. Writers who want to use narrative viewpoints that are extraordinarily naive, mistaken or mendacious also find first-person narrative very useful.

Although a third-person narrative may be tied very intimately to the viewpoint of a particular character, allowing the reader access to that character's private sensations, thoughts and feelings, it still remains an 'objective record'. A first-person narrative retains an essential subjectivity which makes it easier to withhold information from the reader or tell the reader outright lies. If you want to hold back some vital piece of information so that you can spring a surprise on your readers, many of those who might feel cheated if the information were held back by an objective narrative voice may think it more legitimate for a first-person narrator to behave deceptively.

The main disadvantage of using a first-person narrator is that the threats facing them may seem less drastic; they must, after all, have survived or they couldn't be telling the story. (The 'ingenious' switch in which a first-person narrator reveals that he did get killed and is now speaking from beyond the grave no longer seems clever in an era when almost everyone has seen *Sunset Boulevard*.) It is worth remembering, however, that texts employing third-person narrative can easily contain subsidiary first person narratives – perhaps in the form of letters or diaries – and that this allows writers to have it both ways. This option is often used to allow characters who are killed to 'have their own say', heightening their tragedy with an extra measure of intimacy.

The decision whether to use first-person or third-person narrative is largely a matter of personal taste. Some writers love producing first-person narrative and some hate it. Others like to switch back and forth because they like the variety. Some of those who like both will sometimes mix first-person narrative and third-person narrative within a single story, changing voices as they change viewpoint. Some writers who are exceptionally fond of first-person narration even use several different such narrators within a story, although the problem of differentiating between them can become acute. There are few things more likely to confuse a reader than switching from one 'I' to another without making it absolutely clear that such a switch has been made.

If your story requires – or would benefit from – more than one viewpoint the natural thing to do is to lay out a series of third-person narratives, perhaps including some first-person inserts if you want to get the benefit of a little informality, unreliability or added intimacy. If you only intend to use a single viewpoint, the best course may simply be to use whichever seems more comfortable to you, although it might be wise to try out both kinds in different stories until you have learned the kinds of advantages and disadvantages they have.

It is probably safe to say that third-person narrative is now the 'standard' form of popular fiction, and that you have to have a positive reason for using first-person narrative. Although it has not always been my policy, I now tend to confine the use of first-person narrative to stories in which the narrator's attitude and manner of self-expression are part of the subject matter of the story, so that his or her telling of it differs significantly – and interestingly – from a more objective account.

Useful viewpoint characters

Even in a story which has several viewpoint characters they will usually be a small selection of the entire 'cast'. It will often be the case, especially if you are fond of devising idea-as-hero stories, that you will have to decide which of the characters in your story would make the best viewpoint character. In any case, you will have to give some thought to the problem of designing your viewpoint characters in such a way that they will perform that function efficiently.

There is no simple answer to the question of what it is that equips a character to be a really useful viewpoint character. To some extent, obviously, it depends on the nature of the story and the frequency with which particular characters are 'on stage'. Inexperienced writers often make the mistake of using a viewpoint character who is not actually present when vital events occur – thus having to be told about them at second-hand – when it would have been a relatively simple matter to link the reader to a character who is always in the thick of things. There are, however, a number of character types and roles which have great advantages for use as viewpoints.

One of the most useful types of viewpoint character is the innocent abroad: a naive person entering a new environment for the first time. The great advantage of this kind of character is, of course, that the reader can share the innocent's curiosity and wonder, and the innocent can legitimately ask questions whose answers the reader needs to know. In fantasy and science fiction stories set in strange worlds an innocent abroad may be invaluable. Indeed, it may be difficult for the reader to get a firm grip on the story without such a character being provided for identification.

Fantasy and science fiction stories often transplant a character from the known world into the fantasy world to act as a 'carrier' for the reader's own ignorance. This can be convenient for the writer as well as the readers; viewpoint characters are your viewpoint too, and the questions which come into their minds as they confront the exotic scenarios that you lay before them will sometimes be questions whose answers you need to discover in order that you may disclose them. If you are using characters already present in the world within the text, you might find it very helpful to make one of them a child, or a visitor from elsewhere, whose inquiring and sometimes bewildered eye will pick out the things that most need to be explained. The frequent use of children – or Hobbitesque child-substitutes – as main characters in fantasy has as much to do with the necessity of providing a suitable viewpoint as with the popularity of fantasy among the young.

Innocent characters are particularly useful in mystery stories because it is easy for the omniscient author to hide things from them in a plausible manner. In many stories of that kind they fill the role of 'sidekick' to the hero. However useless Dr Watson might have been to Sherlock Holmes as a collaborator in solving problems he was invaluable to Arthur Conan Doyle; because Watson could never see the significance of the clues which revealed everything to Holmes, the solution to every puzzle could be eked out by Doyle in a carefully measured and suitably surprising fashion. If you intend to write a science-fictional mystery you will find it similarly useful to look upon the work of your brilliant scientist from some such angle. If you intend to write a heroic fantasy you might well find it useful to observe the efforts of powerful wizards through the uncomprehending eyes of their clients or apprentices.

One useful variant of the innocent abroad is the anxious victim of cruel circumstance: a character who knows a great deal about the world within the text but cannot understand the particular series of troublesome events in which she is caught up. As such characters react to the unusual things which happen to them they also provide an account of what is to them – but not, of course, to the reader – the usual course of affairs. Managing such characters can be tricky but if it is done cleverly it can smooth out the problems of getting a good deal of information across without crude info-dumps. Philip K. Dick was very fond of employing viewpoint characters of this kind, who usually found the worlds around them becoming inexorably 'curiouser and curiouser'.

A second variant of the innocent abroad, particularly applicable to sidekicks, is the underappreciated helper: a character who makes a considerable contribution to the efforts of others – and hence to the progress of the plot – which usually goes unrecognised and unrewarded. The gap between the character's aspirations and achievements can serve as a margin into which you can introduce useful information, but the resultant frustration is even more valuable as a means of building up narrative tension. Such roles might be particularly appropriate to female characters, for reasons made abundantly clear by James Tiptree Jr's sarcastic science fiction parable 'The Women Men Don't See'.

The main disadvantage of equipping a supremely competent character with a sidekick or some other innocent observer who will serve as the story's viewpoint is that you cannot follow the character on solo expeditions. If your plot requires its heroes to work alone, you may be strongly inclined to make the most competent character the viewpoint character too.

In these circumstances, it makes sense to make the character a deceiver, who has good reasons for keeping his competence secret from the other characters. That way, everything the character does and says will involve an element of concealment. This gives the reader the pleasure of sharing the hero's secret while enabling the writer to conceal things from the reader by allowing the hero to make observations and draw inferences to which no immediate reference need be made in the course of recording his actions or speeches. This is a common tactic in spy stories, whose clever protagonists are often required to work in secret, and it is very useful in fantasy and science fiction stories whose protagonists have good reasons for travelling incognito or operating in disguise. Unusually exaggerated versions of the formula can be found in most superhero comics involving exotic characters with 'secret identities'.

One useful variant of the deceiver is the 'man on the make': a character whose deceptions are organised into a coherent game-plan which will draw out the plot as it develops. People of this kind routinely masquerade as innocents abroad, and are thus able to perform some of the same functions on the writer's behalf. These can be tricky to manage, but they can be very useful as a means of packaging information about the world within the text because the deceiver's accounts of the goals he is trying to attain and the strategies he intends to use can embody a succinct account of the values and social structure of an imaginary society.

Another kind of viewpoint character which can sometimes be useful is the detached observer: a character who is relatively uninvolved with the action of the story but is able to provide a running commentary on that action. This kind of viewpoint character tends, however, to be more attractive to writers than to readers. As a writer you stand outside the action of your story and are in a perfect position to offer a commentary upon it but such a viewpoint is by no means the most engaging to offer to the reader.

Detached observers work best when they are cynical and sarcastic, but many readers find it slightly discomfiting to identify with commentators of that kind. Writers who are cynical and sarcastic themselves may find it impossible to resist the temptation to use such viewpoint characters, but they need to be aware of the risks. Characters who *want* to be detached observers but keep getting caught up in the action in spite of their best evasive efforts are often more useful, especially in comedy. I was once very fond of writing stories of this kind, and my six-volume 'Hooded Swan' series and three-volume 'Asgard' series may serve as examples.

Characterisation

The choice between these various character types and the adaptation of one or more of them to your particular story is, of course, an aspect of the hidden labour of authorship. When planning your story you might find it convenient to think in terms of innocents abroad and detached observers, but what you will offer to your readers is a particular individual, as unique and independent within the world of your text as you are within the world we all inhabit. One of the basic skills of writing is to make your characters seem 'real': to give the impression that they have lives of their own within a world of their own.

The best way of making sure that the world within your text will engage your readers as fully as possible is to make the viewpoint characters' relationships with each other, and with the remaining characters, seem as solid and as vital as the relationships which your reader has with actual people. It is mainly because readers vary so much in the extent, nature and comfort of their actual social relationships that their tastes in reading are so markedly different. One advantage that writers have is that the majority of readers probably find that their relationships with real people are a little unsteady and never as precisely defined as they could wish; they may, in consequence, greatly appreciate the consistency and certainty which writers can bring to the business of characterisation.

There is no simple answer to the question of how much work you need to do in order to make your characters seem real, or what kinds of work you need to do. Some readers are far more demanding in this regard than others, and writers who strive to reach the most exacting standards risk alienating some readers who will find their efforts over-complicated. No writer, however, can get away without paying any attention at all to the business of characterisation. Whether you aim to produce images with the delicacy of fine oil paintings or mere cartoons, your representations must still be *recognisable*.

As I pointed out in chapter 2, the business of characterisation begins with a name. A physical description is optional but is usually helpful; it assists the reader's imagination and allows you to have more than one way to refer to a character. You may well be able to locate your characters within the world of the story simply by specifying their occupations – minor characters who are never named are likely to be identified solely by their jobs or social roles – but in almost all instances you will want to give your reader a sense of the uniqueness of the individual within the occupation, so even the most minimal characterisation tends to couple job descriptions with arbitrary items of distinction: references to height, girth, colour of hair or eyes, and so on.

The more important your characters are, the more elaborate your accounts of them are likely to be. It will sometimes be convenient to offer a detailed physical description, but it is usually more important to construct a personal history for the character. Some writers go to the trouble of constructing elaborate dossiers on their characters, often including more data than they will actually set out within the text. The purpose of this is not so much to help them maintain consistency while composing the story – although it is certainly useful in avoiding 'continuity errors' – but rather to give them a sense of the 'reality' of each character. The more you know about your characters, the easier it may become to present an appearance of reality to your reader. If you know more than your reader does, you may find it much easier to contrive a consistency of attitude and behaviour.

Many writers attempt to construct characters in their own mind by borrowing the physical and behavioural attributes of real people, sometimes straightforwardly but often in combination. If you do this, it is probably wiser – and certainly more diplomatic – to compound characters out of the attributes of several different people rather than basing characters on single real individuals. Your relatives, friends and acquaintances will always look for themselves in your stories, and will very rarely be pleased with whatever they find. It is always advisable to equip each character with a mark of distinction which can be produced as absolute proof that the character in question cannot *possibly* be modelled on your mother, sister or best friend – especially if she is.

As I have previously noted, the advice most often given to experienced writers with regard to establishing characters within a text is 'show, don't tell'. Although it is good, this advice is most pertinent to writers working at a certain level of subtlety. If you want to be on the safe side, you might want to show *and* tell – but it is as well to remember that of the two, showing is the more important. Any character trait which is significant to the plot should always be demonstrated rather than simply recorded.

One of the most effective ways to establish a character in the reader's mind is to present a telling phrase which sums them up, and an exemplary anecdote which underlines the judgment. You might, for instance, introduce a spoilt brat by means of another character's ironically overstated observation that 'he's the kind of kid who expects Daddy to turn off the rain'; if such an observation can be swiftly backed up by an incident in which the boy in question has an employee sacked for some trivial and altogether understandable slight that will enable the reader to bring the loathsome lad much more sharply into focus.

The 'show, don't tell' rule needs to be accompanied by some notion of what it is that needs to be shown. Many characters can be adequately established by deft reference to a single outstanding virtue or a single outstanding vice, and there are some kinds of fast-moving popular fiction which may be handicapped in their flow if anything more than that is done. Important characters, however, usually require more detail. As well as identifying cardinal virtues and vices it is a good idea to offer some account of personal idiosyncrasies: habits of speech, behaviour and consumption, and particular areas of interest. Characters may only require initial identification in terms of their jobs, but they can be made into better-rounded individuals by reference to their families, their hobbies and their lifestyles.

Characterisation in fantasy and science fiction

Writers who use known-world settings have certain advantages when introducing their readers to their characters. At a trivial level, characters operating in fictional worlds identical to our own can readily be summed up in terms of the shops they patronise, the newspapers they read, the TV programmes they watch, the music they like and the sports they follow. None of these identifiers are available with respect to characters who inhabit distant futures or secondary-worlds.

This difficulty would be troublesome enough if it only involved mere matters of apparatus, but in fact it cuts more deeply than that. What you will usually be displaying in the exemplary anecdotes which allow your readers to get your characters into focus is their interaction with other characters. Characterisation is not so much a matter of detailing the individual psychology of characters as detailing the manner in which they relate to others. In a world markedly different from our own, social relationships are apt to be organised in a different way, regulated by a markedly different etiquette.

This does not reduce the importance of exemplary anecdotes in characterisation, but it does mean that the significance of the exemplary anecdotes may be much less easy for the reader to grasp. The things you show must introduce the world within your text as well as the characters, and the reader's understanding of that world *and* those characters must proceed in tandem.

A viewpoint character who is displaced from the known world may be characterised before displacement, but that does not lessen the difficulty of characterising individuals who belong entirely to exotic worlds within texts. The viewpoint character may echo the bewilderment of the reader, but the writer still needs to do the work of telling and showing – of making the characters make sense in their own terms so that they may then make sense to the reader.

One of the principal accusations levelled against writers of fantasy and science fiction by disapproving critics is that their characterisation is inept. To the extent that this is so, it has far more to do with the intrinsic difficulties posed by the genres than with the skill of the writers. It is, of course, open to critically ambitious writers to specialise in those kinds of fantasy and science fiction which can be set in the known world – in the present, the past or the imminent future – so that they can take advantage of all the apparatus of ready characterisation that the known world offers, but not everyone wants to do that and it might be regarded by some critics as cowardly.

Those bold explorers who do want to venture into farther futures and stranger parallel worlds will benefit if they make their human characters as accessible as possible, even if the opportunity to do that is restricted. Even writers who carefully retain all the advantages in dealing with their human characters will occasionally have to deal with non-human characters if they are not to restrict themselves to a handful of marginal sub-genres of the fantasy and science fiction fields.

This problem is awkward, but writers of fantasy and science fiction do have advantages as well as disadvantages. It is sometimes easier for readers to imagine themselves in the shoes of a non-human character than those of a human. Young readers inexperienced in the business of social interaction may find such a step very tempting as well as easy, and many adults can find a special relief in identifying with a simpler kind of being.

Everyday social life requires a conformity to the expectations of others that often becomes burdensome, if not outrightly oppressive, and texts which allow us to remove ourselves entirely to alien environments can be very appealing. It is worth bearing in mind that some texts may be attractive to some readers precisely because within them minutely accurate characterisation is impossible.

Characterising non-humans

There are two possible approaches to characterising non-humans. One involves starting with a 'blank space' and filling in attributes as required; the other involves starting with a human being and either adding or subtracting some highly significant attribute which serves to define the modified individual as unhuman. The latter approach is much easier, and consequently far more common.

Anyone familiar with science fiction will be well aware of certain clichéd kinds of characterisation by subtraction. Robots and other artificial intelligences are routinely characterised by a lack of emotion, which is often assumed to make them both 'perfectly rational' and amoral. The same tactic is frequently used in characterising superhumans and aliens. This has something to do with the fact that we often see ourselves as significantly divided, with a rational and moral 'higher' self constantly struggling to subdue a 'lower' self dominated by appetites and passions, and are also aware of a division of interest between rationality and morality. Non-human entities which have achieved a total or partial settlement of this internal war are of special interest to us.

One of the significant differences between science fiction and fantasy is the way in which they usually employ the tactics of subtraction. Although genre fantasy does make use of dispassionate characters – wizards are often characterised by some such strategy – it makes far more use of characters in which rationality is diminished relative to the forces of appetite and emotion. Thus, while science fiction tends to thrust the conflict between reason and morality into the foreground, fantasy tends to bring the conflict between morality and passion to the fore.

The most common internal attributes which are added to characters in fantasy and science fiction are strikingly similar in both genres, although they may be described in different jargon terms. While fantasy speaks of magical powers, science fiction may speak of ESP or invoke mechanical aids, but the abilities thus gifted fill much the same range. Mind-reading, foreseeing the future, moving objects (often including oneself) by the power of the mind and making oneself invisible are the most familiar. Given that these are commonplace wishes, it is not surprising that both genres should be interested in fantasies of their fulfilment, although fantasy can approach them more directly and more frankly than science fiction.

Whether you are adding or subtracting mental attributes to your characters, the business of characterisation is a matter of extrapolation and correlation. You need to ask yourself what else would change, and how, if characters were gifted with particular advantages or handicapped by particular lacks. How would it affect their behaviour, their attitude to others, their interests, their lifestyles? If you choose to deal with a whole race of non-humans rather than an individual you must ask what effects the alteration would have on their society – and hence, perhaps, on the entire world within your text. In this respect, creating non-human characters is closely akin to dealing with any other kind of novum, and the examination of a particular interaction between human and non-human characters may indeed be your heroic idea.

The addition and subtraction of internal attributes is often correlated with external differences. In designing alien beings, science fiction writers tend to start with modifications of appearance – replacing some or all of the basics of human form with characteristics borrowed from other living species – and then do their best to extrapolate appropriate mental differences.

Fantasy writers are much more likely than science fiction writers to alter external appearances while maintaining internal ones; indeed, there are whole sub-genres of fantasy which employ calculated anthropomorphism, equipping animals with human-like thoughts, emotions and powers of speech. In modern fantasies, however, most writers do take care to pay some attention to the ways in which the world view of a non-human creature, whether it be a rabbit, a dragon or an elemental, might be expected to diverge from that of a human.

Again, the problem which faces you as a writer is one of extrapolation and correlation. If your alien beings are supposed to be descended from spiders or gazelles instead of apes, then they should look upon other beings as spiders or gazelles would. In this instance, character-isation is partly a matter of ecology; the mind-set of a predator would presumably be considerably different from the mind-set of a herbi-vore, an omnivore or a parasite. Science fiction writers have, of course, been very interested in modelling aliens on creatures which have unusual life-cycles and unusual social organisations: ants and bees have always exerted a particular fascination on writers interested in characterising whole alien societies, from the Selenites in H. G. Wells's *The First Men in the Moon* to the Buggers of Orson Scott Card's *Ender's Game*.

It is still possible for both fantasy and science fiction writers to get away with offering supposedly non-human characters who are merely humans in fancy dress, but is a lazy way to approach the job. Unfortunately, even the writer who conscientiously extrapolates a complicated set of attributes which serves to differentiate an entire alien species from humanity still has to put further work into charac-terising particular individuals within that species. Equipping non-human characters with their own idiosyncrasies is bound to be more awkward than equipping human characters with their own individu-ality because it is far more difficult to contrive exemplary anecdotes with which to reveal the telling details. This is a job which can only be fudged – you just have to fudge it as best you can.

Characters larger than life

A famous literary critic of my acquaintance once responded to a ques-tion about the people in Shakespeare's plays by saying, witheringly: 'There are no *people* in Shakespeare's plays; there are only *narrative devices'*. The person who asked the question was devastated; he had grown used to thinking of the characters in Shakespeare's plays as if they were every bit as real as people he knew – and considerably *more* real than some.

The critic is, of course, correct. The characters in stories are no more than narrative devices cunningly contrived by writers. There is a sense, however, in which we ourselves are self-made narrative devices. The appearances we offer to the world are performances, characters we labour long and hard to produce, and even within the privacy of our own minds we understand ourselves in terms of our 'life stories'. It is no wonder, therefore, that the best characters in fiction, forged by the cleverest writers, sometimes seem *more* real than real people, larger than life.

We are all familiar with the strange sense of intimacy we may develop with our favourite characters in fiction. Actors who play characters in popular TV soap operas have to become accustomed to the fact that wherever they go people will think they know them, quite forgetting that the 'person' they 'know' is a fiction entirely separate from the actor. We may easily come to feel that we know certain fictional characters far better than we know our actual friends and relatives – for the simple reason that we really *do* know them far better. No matter how well we know our friends, there is an important sense in which they remain inaccessible and unfathomable, but characters in books have no secrets from us; what we read on the page is everything that there is to know about them.

One of the greatest attainments a writer can achieve is to create a character who seems more real to a substantial number of readers than any actual individual. It might be a character that we could look up to as a role model, or it might be a character who comes to symbolise something we loathe. Given the choice, most writers would rather create a memorable hero than a memorable villain, but the latter achievement might be reckoned more considerable simply because it is rarer. For every Dracula there is a whole gaggle of Tarzans – and Dracula needed only one book and one film to become *the* vampire, whereas Tarzan required a whole series of each.

Not all writers want to create characters of extraordinary magnitude; many are happy forging a different cast for each of their stories. Many writers are attracted to fantasy and science fiction, however, because it is those genres which most readily play host to great heroes and great villains. Indeed, any character in fiction who attains that status begins to move his oeuvre towards the margins of fantasy; in becoming mythic themselves great heroes and great villains make the worlds in which they operate mythic too.

There are few problems faced by the inexperienced writer quite as daunting as creating heroes and villains. The easiest way to solve the problem is to clone somebody else's hero or villain, and it is an option which many writers take. Indeed, it is now commonplace for notable heroes to become common property, shared between a whole team of writers. The obvious fact that both cloning and sharing can provide launching pads for huge commercial success encourages such practices, to the extent that they now provide the core marketplace of both fantasy and science fiction.

If you intend to create new adventures for pre-existent heroes, or close imitations thereof, you will find that much of the work of characterisation has already been done for you. The 'bibles' which conserve the lore of various shared-world enterprises will normally contain elaborate dossiers on the key characters, and if you are imitating you will be able to base your own dossiers on ones distilled from your models. This will not free you from the need to include exemplary anecdotes, but it will subtly change the purpose of such anecdotes; what you are 'showing' is that your cast is, indeed, composed of characters the reader already knows and loves – or characters so similar to other characters the reader already knows and loves that ease of acquaintance and lovability are guaranteed.

If you are interested in this kind of work you must pay close attention to matters of copyright and trademark law. If you intend to use other people's characters you must do so under licence; all new Doctor Who novels and Tarzan novels have to be commissioned by the copyright holders and it is to them that you must submit your proposals. Some characters have been around so long that they have fallen unambiguously into the public domain – Dracula is one – but others remain in a problematic situation which has been further compounded by the recent extension of British copyright protection to seventy years after an author's death rather than fifty. Sherlock Holmes, who was in the public domain in Britain when I published the serial version of *The Hunger and Ecstasy of Vampires*, was re-copyrighted by the change in the law.

Fantastic adventure stories set in the nineteenth century, usually mingling well-known fictional characters with real historical individuals have recently become fashionable enough to earn the sub-genre label 'steampunk'. It is sometimes necessary for writers of such stories to disguise some of the characters in them. For example, in Kim Newman's *Anno Dracula* there is a character who is obviously Sax Rohmer's Fu Manchu, but cannot be named. If you are interested in writing this kind of fiction you must be careful. The use of real people is controlled by the law of libel rather than by copyright law and the dead cannot be libelled, but if you want to borrow somebody else's characters you *must* obtain permission, unless the creator has been dead more than seventy years.

Imitating other people's heroes is free of copyright control, so you are free to produce clones of any characters you like, provided that you give them different names. Few writers approve of this sort of imitative exercise but many of them do it anyway. Everyone, however, holds in far higher regard those rare writers who contrive to break the old moulds and establish new heroes or new villains. There is, of course, no simple recipe for doing that, but it is worth noting that the new heroes and villains which do spring to pre-eminence over all competitors are those who carry some particular mental attribute to the limit and also embody some crucial aspect of their historical moment.

The need to adapt heroes to present-day concerns may seem slightly odd, given that heroism is often expressed in purely physical terms and that heroes often operate in fictional worlds very remote from the known worlds of their readers, but it is true nevertheless. If you want to create new heroes you need to define their world-view in such a way that it echoes something new in the known world and you need to design their world so that it echoes something newly significant in the known world. For instance, Miles Vorkosigan – the hero of a recent multi-award-winning series of science fiction novels by Lois McMaster Bujold – compensates for his physical deficiencies with a cunning admixture of native intelligence and mechanical assistance; he is remarkably well-tailored to the tangled politics and rapidly advancing medical cyborgisation of the present day.

The same principle applies, perhaps more obviously, to new villains: they must embody, somehow, an anxiety which has lately become more powerful in the known world. All Dark Lords symbolise evil, but a canny creator of Dark Lords needs to keep an ear to the ground in order to detect the constant subtle shifts which affect known-world ideas of what evil is, how it manifests itself, and why.

One effect of these kinds of shifts is that yesterday's villains may become tomorrow's heroes (and, more rarely, *vice versa*). Modern heroes are almost invariably flawed in some way, because one of the things they reflect is that we are much more doubtful nowadays about what actually constitutes heroism and how practical heroism is as a vocation. When designing and displaying heroes, it is worth devoting at least as much time to the display of their flaws as to the display of their strengths – you will, in any case, want to save their best shot for the climax of your story.

It is as well to remember that fantasy and science fiction stories are not stocked entirely with extraordinary characters and that writers ambitious to work in these genres still need to know how to characterise ordinary people. Some advisors – especially those interested in the more rigorous forms of science fiction – will argue that the most artful imaginative fiction is that which places perfectly ordinary people in very extraordinary situations. There is, however, much to be gained by developing your skills in the characterisation of extraordinary individuals, whether they are to be fitted to their own extraordinary worlds or set free within the known world.

6

'SO, WHAT HAPPENED, EXACTLY?': DIALOGUE AND EXPOSITION

Content and style

Everything that I have discussed so far can be grouped together as the 'content' of the story, as contrasted to its 'style'. Content and style are not really separable in this way, because every alteration of content affects the style, and vice versa, but there is some sense in making the distinction. The content of a story is its 'inside' while the style is its 'outside', and we look at them as differently as we look at the insides and outsides of human beings. We generally think of insides in terms of function and outsides in terms of appearance; it is the surfaces of stories that we examine aesthetically rather than their cores.

The surface of a story consists of a flow of words, chosen and arranged in the interests of elegance. There are many different ways in which this might be achieved, none of which can easily be reduced to matters of mere calculation. There are, however, certain features of narrative surfaces which are worth investigative analysis. The most obvious differentiation to be made in looking at a narrative surface is between dialogue and exposition – put crudely, the bits within the speech marks and the rest. Some stories are almost all dialogue, others almost all exposition, but most try to strike a balance between the two. Getting this balance right is not easy.

Some inexperienced writers find it difficult to produce naturalistic dialogue and therefore shy away from it, while others find the flow of conversation so congenial that they have to make a concerted effort to attack the work of describing what is happening and filling in background information. Writers of the first kind tend to produce stories in which the contents of conversations are frequently reported to the reader in a summary fashion. (They talked for hours. Sue told Mark about a strange woman she had met, who stopped her in the street and told her that she ought to look out because...). Writers of the other persuasion tend to produce stories in which the reader is informed about everything that happens entirely by what people say about it. ('So, what happened, exactly?' 'Well, we were driving along the A303 and we suddenly saw this bright light.' 'Up in the sky?' 'Yeah way up high – at first I thought nothing of it, but then...')

There is nothing intrinsically wrong with either of these tactics and both methods of presentation can be useful. Because either of them can be used to condense information both are frequently employed in short fiction; very short stories usually consist almost entirely of summary reportage or almost entirely of dialogue. There is, however, considerable advantage to be obtained from making your dialogue and exposition do what each is best equipped to do, so that they may work as a team in shaping and polishing the surface of your narrative.

Dialogue and characterisation

First and foremost, the dialogue in your story ought to be the primary vehicle of characterisation. It has to be, given that in real life, conversation is the principal means that people employ to 'characterise' themselves.

The crudest of all methods of story characterisation involves making lower-class characters say ''ow are ya?' and 'darlin'', making effete aesthetes exclaim 'I thay!' and making French speakers use 'ze' instead of 'the'. Such devices do serve the function of letting the reader know who is speaking but they are so crude that they are mostly confined to comedy and the most elementary action/adventure fiction.

The usefulness of regional accents in more sophisticated work depends on your ability to give them an appropriate phonetic form. Producing an 'eye-dialect' which the reader can comfortably follow is by no means easy. This problem has a further complexity in those kinds of fantasy and science fiction story which deal with non-human beings. It makes sense to have non-human beings speak in a non-human way and they will hardly be convincing aliens if they do not. Dialogues between humans and science-fictional aliens are a veritable minefield for the writer; there is a very thin line separating eye-dialects and speech impediments which are not peculiar enough to seem authentically alien from ones which are so peculiar as to be horribly difficult to write or read.

The best opportunities for characterisation through dialogue have less to do with mannerisms than with preoccupations. Different people have different agendas, in terms of what interests them and what they are trying to achieve, and these agendas affect what they say and how. In real life, people are always talking, at least to some slight degree, at cross purposes. Very few actual conversations are straight-forward exchanges of information, and even the ones that are involve a significant element of performance. Most real-world conversations are part social ritual and part competition.

Dialogue in stories, however 'realistic' it is intended to seem, has to be very different from real conversation because its true function is to convey information to the reader. Story dialogue is much more concerned with the exchange of information and much less concerned with mere social ritual than actual dialogue, but it retains the elements of performance and competition. It is through these aspects of the story dialogue that your characters can and should express themselves, thus defining themselves as individuals, and push forward their competing agendas, thus helping to move your story along.

In fantasy and science fiction, mannerisms of speech may lose much of the meaning they have in known-world fiction, but the importance of speech as a means of characterisation is not diminished. If anything, it is increased. Spoken catch-phrases may become the keys by which exotic characters are identified and summed up. These may be straightforwardly reflective of the character's nature – as 'That does not compute' is of the robot in *Lost in Space* – but they may be more oblique.

The competitive element of conversation is often a matter of trying to seem competent and clever, although anyone acquainted with the

intimate politics of family life will know that people also compete –
often very fiercely – in matters of affection ('You wouldn't do that if
you really loved me'), concern ('I'm only doing it because I care about
you'), propriety ('She's such a slut') and fortitude ('That's nothing –
when I had *my* operation...'). You can often define your characters
accurately and distinctly by taking a little trouble to disclose the kinds
of competition in which they like to indulge and the level of skill which
they bring into their verbal combat.

It is true that none of your characters can be more skilled in conversational competition than you are, but your characters can have the
benefit of your second thoughts. We all know how much easier it is to
be brilliant when we replay conversations in our minds, substituting
the lines we could have used to devastating effect, if only we'd thought
of them at the time. Indeed, by working hard on your characters you
should be able to improve and refine your own conversational skills. It
might require an Oscar Wilde to produce literary conversation as brilliant as that in *The Picture of Dorian Gray*, but if he had not lavished
such careful attention on the characters in his literary works even
Oscar Wilde might have remained a pale shadow of the self he eventually made.

The most common fault that inexperienced writers display in
constructing dialogue is that their characters confine themselves to
ritual greetings and the communication of information, neglecting the
elements of performance and competition. Dialogue which simply
consists of one character informing another of matters relevant to the
plot is bound to seem flat and stilted. Some inexperienced writers try
to solve this problem by trying to make their dialogues seem more like
actual dialogues, but if you try to do that by importing more of the
purely ritual aspects of real-world dialogue – remarks about the
weather, polite questions which are not really meant to be answered,
and so on – you may make matters worse instead of better.

You can only enliven the dialogue in your stories by making it more
expressive and more competitive, and if your characters are to 'come
to life' on the page their habits of speech will play a major role in
giving them the necessary vitality.

Dialogue and explanation

Story dialogue is a very useful vehicle for communicating information – so much so that there are forms of fiction in which everything the reader needs to know is revealed through conversation. Many detective stories are little more than a series of interrogations punctuated by reflective sequences in which the detective and his sidekick sort through the evidence side by side, piecing together the answer to the puzzle.

Because the worlds within science fiction and fantasy texts often need elaborate explanation the dialogue in fantastic stories is frequently required to carry a heavy load of information. You have to bear in mind, however, that an info-dump within speech marks is still an info-dump. Having one of your characters deliver a long lecture on the history leading up to your hypothetical future, or on the particular backwater of Egyptian mythology in which you discovered the monster currently harassing your hero, can be just as indigestible as any expository lump. Such a device looks even clumsier if it is obvious to the reader that the character has no reason for delivering the lecture except to get the information across to the reader. If you ever find one of your characters beginning a long explanatory speech with the words 'As you know...', it is time to stop and think about better ways of getting the information across.

One of the great advantages of having an 'innocent abroad' as your main character – or one of your main characters – is that such characters need to find out what is going on. They can ask questions, and they have a legitimate reason for sitting through explanatory lectures. It is often a good move to make sure that your cast of characters also includes a 'wise old man' who can, at some point, sit down with your innocent abroad and explain to him exactly what is going on and why. If you adopt this strategy, however, it is usually a good move to delay that explanatory lecture until the last possible moment. While your central character and your reader still have interesting questions to ask your plot still has that extra measure of dramatic tension – and if you can arrange events so that the questions become increasingly urgent the intractability of the mystery will help prepare the way for your climax.

Inexperienced writers often bring on their wise old man far too soon for good dramatic effect. This is an understandable temptation, because having wise old men explain things often helps writers get their arguments straight in their own minds – we all know the feeling of not knowing exactly what we think until we have actually spelled it out. A less obvious but equally common error is to have an ever-present wise old man who stubbornly refuses to answer questions until the climax – at which point it becomes painfully obvious that he could have saved everyone a great deal of trouble had he only revealed what he knew much sooner. This is why so many fantasy novels bring their greatest wizards on stage at the beginning, to get the plot moving, but then remove them from the action until the want of their wisdom becomes desperate.

One great advantage of using dialogue rather than exposition to communicate information about the world within the text is that it is much easier to break up the info-dumps into convenient pieces. Ideally, the dialogue which serves this purpose will still be performing the functions outlined above, so that there can and should be an element of verbal combat in the encounter between the innocent and the wise old man. A fervent interrogation peppered with objections and accusations is far more lively than a lecture, but will still do the job of getting the information into the text. An insistent lecturer whose target keeps unsuccessfully trying to escape from him can also get a great deal of information across without the story losing its momentum.

When thinking about how best to get information across to your reader, you should remember that learning is not simply a matter of being told. Dialogue was originally a kind of philosophical discourse, developed by Socrates and Plato, and a means of working through a problem. Writing fantasy and science fiction tends to bring writers into contact with philosophical questions, even if they are only trying to produce colourful and fast-paced action/adventure stories. The use of magic inevitably raises questions of morality and metaphysics, while attempts to extrapolate possible futures and believable alien worlds require constant analytical argument. Such questions can often be clarified, and partially worked through, in dialogue.

There is a sub-genre of fiction called the *conte philosophique* – the French term is used because the most striking early examples were produced by Voltaire – which uses fiction to explore philosophically interesting questions, frequently employing fantasy and science fiction devices in order to do so. If you intend to write serious fantasy and science fiction your work will inevitably be infected by an element of *conte philosophique*, and your characters are likely to bounce ideas off each other even if you have no intention to get a specific 'message' across to your readers.

Inexperienced writers tend to rush into enquiring dialogues as well as info-dumping ones, and even experienced ones may find themselves continually getting sidetracked because their characters digress in this fashion. Until you get your story's key ideas into written form you may not be sure in your own mind what questions need to be brought into sharp focus and what conclusions, if any, you ought to come to. For the sake of dramatic tension and narrative flow, though, it is usually best to save such inquiries until your story has built up enough momentum and pressure to carry the reader through them with relative ease.

As with cleverness and wit, your characters can never manifest more knowledge or philosophical acuity in their dialogues than you actually possess. As with cleverness and wit, however, you will never know how much you can learn or how much you can reason out unless you practise. Trying to write better stories will actually help you to become more intelligent, and the more intelligent you become the better the stories will be that you are able to write.

There is no guarantee that writing fantasy and science fiction will do more for your intellectual development than any other kind of fiction, but observations of my fellow-writers in those genres suggest that it can certainly help you to *believe* that you have become unusually clever.

Dialogue structure

Whatever functions you are using dialogue to perform, it needs to be structured. One of the most common worries afflicting inexperienced writers is how often to use the word 'said', and this problem is less trivial than it may seem.

It is a good idea to identify the speaker of most of the items of dialogue in your story. You do not have to do this for *every* act of speech, especially if the context makes it obvious – if, for instance, one person is asking a series of questions and the other is providing straightforward answers – but if you let two or three exchanges go by without 'posting flags' of the 'he said/she said' kind your reader may become confused. Because *you* always know who is saying what, it is easy for you to underestimate the number of flags required to keep your reader in the picture.

The problem with flagging all or most items of dialogue is that the flags soon come to seem irritatingly repetitive. This problem is not as bad as it sometimes seems to the writer because readers do not give equal attention to every word in the text and the flags are usually registered so faintly that repetition of the word 'said' is much less obvious and much less awkward than other repetitions. Even so, various strategies are commonly employed in the cause of making the repetition seem even less awkward.

Some writers substitute other words for 'said' as often as they can, so that their characters are forever muttering, exclaiming, snarling, shouting, and so forth. Used in moderation, such substitutions can, of course, make dialogue more expressive, but when they are used to excess they can become slightly absurd. Some writers become so desperate to avoid the word 'said' that they begin using substitutes that do not actually describe acts of speech at all, so that words like 'shrugged' are inappropriately drafted and cab drivers reporting to their controllers may be charged with 'radioing'. Some readers can filter out such devices as easily as they can filter out the elementary flags, but others find them jarring.

Another way to make repetitions of 'said' seem less awkward is to modify the word with adverbs. This is, I confess, my own reflexive response to the problem. My characters rarely just say things; they are forever saying things softly, resentfully, off-handedly, assertively, and so on. This too can become slightly absurd. It can also get you involved in fierce disputes with copy editors as to whether or not the 'said' and the adverb ought or ought not to be separated by a comma.

It is easy to make fun of either of these strategies ('There are no flowers here,' he said, lackadaisically/'I can do anything a man can do!' she ejaculated) but it takes a strong will to stick relentlessly to the unmodified said. Nor does the problem end there, because the names of the characters who are speaking repeat along with the verb. If your conversationalists are of opposite sex you can break the pattern by substituting pronouns for the names, but if they are both of the same sex 'he said' and 'she said' can no longer function as flags. In order to avoid repeating the names of speakers it is useful, if not absolutely necessary, to have a few substitutes ready. If you are to use such flags as 'the younger man said' and 'the redhead said' you have to be sure that your reader does know which of the men is the younger and which of the women has the red hair.

Much dialogue in fiction consists entirely of speech and flags that identify the speakers, almost as if the reader were listening to it on the radio. Such dialogues may take place while the characters are sitting down or walking along, at intervals in the story's action. It helps to maintain narrative flow, however, if people are doing something while they talk. If the dialogue can be interwoven with a commentary on what the speakers are doing, that can help considerably to relieve the oppressive repetition of the dialogue flags. If you try to introduce such a commentary with the sole aim of breaking up the dialogue, however, you may find yourself inventing actions which are empty of significance. If your characters are forever fiddling with cigarettes or taking another sip from their glasses of wine that too can become awkward and irritating. It is always best, if you can, to interweave your dialogues with actions which actually carry the story forward.

There is one kind of 'action' which your viewpoint character can carry out while engaging in dialogue which warrants special mention, and that is thinking. It is worth remembering that real-world speech is often deceptive, if only because it is controlled by codes of politeness which prevent people from saying what they really think. Every dialogue therefore has a 'hidden' component – we are all familiar with TV comedy routines which superimpose a voice-over or set of subtitles representing two characters' private thoughts upon their actual speeches, revealing the extent of their dishonesty.

Dialogue enlivened by conflict can sometimes be further enlivened by adding this extra layer of secret commentary to the viewpoint character's observations and responses. The viewpoint character is thus able to react twice to what the other person says and does, what she says out loud being a tactical response based on a private judgment. When your dialogue has to convey a lot of information to the reader – as it will often have to do in a fantasy or science fiction story – it is sometimes helpful to be able to distribute it between thought and speech.

The conventional way to represent thoughts framed in words is to italicise them, but if your story is required to make unusually extravagant use of 'silent speech' you may need to devise conventions of your own. If, for instance, your characters can communicate telepathically, you may need to distinguish between private thoughts and 'transmitted thoughts' by recruiting long dashes or indents. This may be one instance in which the use of different fonts within your story may become desirable, or even necessary.

Description

The principal function of the expository part of your story is description. Many writers pay particular attention to the description of the various settings in which their stories take place, thus helping their readers to 'visualise' the narrative. Some readers appreciate this assistance but others do not. This is because people differ very widely in the manner of their reading, some converting texts into 'internal films' while others consume them 'raw', as strings of words. People differ quite markedly in the extent to which they use words and visual images in their everyday thought processes, and this necessarily affects the way they read.

The logic of the situation suggests that writers are, on average, more disposed to think in words than readers, although readers will, on average, be more inclined to think in words than people who do not like to read. You may, therefore, be inclined to underestimate the extent to which your 'average reader' requires assistance in converting your words into pictures. Because writers and readers vary so much in their interest in and reliance on visual images there is no simple answer to the question of how much description you need to include in your stories. The sensible course is to do what seems most comfortable to you, while bearing in mind that including no description at all will certainly alienate some readers, while providing very elaborate descriptions will probably put off some others. The best compromise may be to use descriptions which are as brief as they can be while still providing sufficient support for the reader's imagination.

In much the same way that a good memory is one which is adept at forgetting all the trivia while retaining only the important data, a good descriptive style is one which leaves out all the unnecessary observations while providing effective imaginative cues. The power of suggestion is enormously valuable to a writer; ideally, you ought to give the impression of having conveyed a good deal of information even when you have merely sketched in a few telling details.

The settings of your story are not the only things that may require description. You will also need to provide descriptions of the characters, especially if you want to use aspects of physical description when flagging their dialogue. You will certainly have to describe their actions, especially when they become involved in dramatic incidents like fights, chases, unfortunate mishaps and so on. You may also need to describe their feelings as they react and respond to the events of the story.

All these kinds of description raise particular tactical problems with respect to the language of the description and the way in which it is deployed. In all cases, though, there is a spectrum of methods which extends from description by dossier to description by impression. At one extreme of this spectrum the description will provide a list of individual items of observation which the reader can assemble into an overall picture ('He was six feet tall with neatly trimmed brown hair and blue eyes. He was dressed in a grey Armani suit and he was carrying a copy of the *Financial Times*...'). At the other extreme, the description will provide statements of similarity and difference which may be very vague indeed, substituting colourful wordplay for accurate specification ('He looked as if he had just stepped out of an ad for Calvin Klein's *Obsession*, with a smile like a freshly stropped razor...').

Description often has to do more than convey information. In worlds within texts, places and objects are often symbolic, carrying an extra layer of meaning over and above their mere presence. Indeed, the choice of which items of the story's environment are brought into sharp focus depends almost entirely on their relevance to the plot and their symbolic value. If an object has neither, it may be best not to lavish too much attention on it, or even to refrain from recording its presence at all. The symbolic significance of an object usually determines the way in which it is described, especially if it is to be described in terms of its likeness to something else.

Although the French writers of the late nineteenth century who are nowadays called Symbolists were by no means the first writers to use symbols in their work they did make the techniques of symbolism far more blatant. Many of them were especially fond of the symbolism of flowers, whose common names often embody ready-made symbolic meanings: narcissus, forget-me-not, passion-flower, venus fly-trap, and so on. Other favourite symbolic devices include timepieces (stopped clocks, burning candles, tolling bells, and so forth) and works of art (accusative portraits, significantly decorated wallpaper, books whose plots are echoed in the story, etc). It is the way that such objects are described within your text that builds piquant patterns of connection and resonance within your stories – patterns which can add tensile strength to your plot-threads and may even replace plots entirely.

Describing places and people

I have already given some consideration to the description of settings in chapter 1, when I talked about the need to make worlds within texts coherent and to locate them in relation to the known world. I pointed out then that the 'authority' of the writer – which determines the willingness of readers to accept and trust what they are being told – is partly dependent on the accuracy with which places already known to both writer and reader are described. Getting such descriptions right involves not merely avoiding errors but also focusing on the most revealing matters of detail – the ones which best 'capture the essence' of the place in question.

It is as well when hunting for telling details to remember that there are five senses. A place might be characterised as much by its typical sounds and odours as by visual details. Even sensations of taste and touch might be evoked, given that air is rarely still and never empty. Indeed, of all the aspects of a story which can be pressed into service as symbols, weather is the most versatile, and perhaps the most useful. In much the same way that people have incorporated symbols in giving names to flowers, people contemplating the weather have always tended to adopt the language of emotion, thus creating the 'pathetic fallacy' by which storms are seen as Nature's wrath and warm sunny days as the world's contentment.

In the worlds within texts, the weather incorporated into descriptions of the story's settings is very often symbolic of the moods of the characters or the state of the plot; this has been particularly true of fantastic fictions ever since the heyday of the emotionally extravagant Gothic novel. Edward Bulwer-Lytton's *Paul Clifford*, whose oft-mocked opening paragraph begins 'It was a dark and stormy night...' was not a fantasy, but G. P. R. James's *The Castle of Ehrenstein*, which begins 'It was an exceedingly dark and tempestuous night...' was. It is in fantasy and science fiction that we find the darkest shadows and the brightest lights.

The imaginary settings of fantasy and science fiction pose particular problems for writers. Many secondary worlds are similar to the known world and most hypothetical futures retain the majority of its features, but the significant features of such worlds are those which make them different and it is these which the writer must get across to the readers. The most obvious problem which faces you as you begin the work of establishing the fantastic aspects of the world within your text is that of naming. If your story is set in an alien world then every town and every river, every plant and every animal ought – in theory, at least – to require a name of its own, and all such names must be invented. Place names can often be borrowed – much as place names in America and Australia often recapitulate European place names, sometimes with the prefix 'New' – and animals can often be named by modifying or combining the names of known-world animals, but if you refrain from making up any new words at all your descriptions may not seem sufficiently exotic. The problem is, of course, compounded by the necessity of naming your characters.

Attaching names to characters is always a problem. Many writers keep 'stocks' of names handy, returning to the telephone directory every now and again to strip-mine a few more. Even if you are using known-world settings, however, it may be a good idea to use slightly unusual names and it is certainly a good idea to avoid using the names of real people, lest you should run foul of the law of libel. The more exotic your characters are the more exotic their names ought to be, although it is sometimes possible to run a double bluff by giving bizarre alien creatures bathetically familiar names. Standard techniques for framing sets of alien names include the liberal use of apostrophes and the consistent use of unusual consonant formations, although both devices irritate those readers who like their eye-dialects to be easily pronounceable. Giving a dolphin a name like 'Kjwalll'kje'k'koothaïlll'kje'k, as Roger Zelazny once did, will undoubtedly seem convincing and evocative to some readers, but if a story requires a whole school of dolphins it might be sensible to choose names that are a little less intimidating.

It is unfortunately easy for descriptions in fantasy and science fiction stories to fill up with words which have no meaning except the ones you assign to them. Each word you invent will have to be defined, and providing such definitions may turn even simple descriptions into bloated info-dumps. You also have to bear in mind that your readers will have to remember all the invented words and their definitions, and may become impatient if they have to keep flicking back through the pages to remind themselves which word means what. Some texts cope with this problem forthrightly by including a glossary, but readers may resent continually having to interrupt the flow of a text in order to seek such assistance.

Many words are, of course, sufficiently general to be easily transferred to fantastic contexts. A secondary-world is likely to have trees and flowers even if they are not the same trees and flowers that the known world has, and you may not need to invent more than a few new terms for individual species. It is often the case that you can build descriptions of fantastic worlds simply by putting familiar words and parts of words into unfamiliar combinations, deriving the names of exotic animals and plants by the chimerical combination of actual animal names. For instance, my three-decker novel *Genesys* is replete with lizardlions, gemsnakes, gaudtrees, dragomites (half-dragon, half-termite!), hellhounds and so on. Unfortunately, such formulations often seem to have a kind of built-in absurdity which may make them seem comical even if they are not intended to be. The characterisation of aliens as 'little green men' has become a running joke, like flying pigs.

The hypothetical machines of science fiction can often be defined simply by function. Time machines, starships, blasters and matter transporters are self-explanatory, as cloaks of invisibility and seven-league boots are in fantasy. Even so, science fiction gradually developed a jargon of its own, some of which has been fed back into actual usage as the known world has caught up with fiction, 'robot' being the most celebrated example. Useful terms invented by one writer are often borrowed by others – for instance, several writers now use communication devices called 'ansibles' and talk of 'terraforming' alien worlds has become commonplace. The integration of such terms into science-fictional description can pose problems for writers unused to the conventions of the field and descriptions which are too heavily laden with such jargon – especially if some words are used inappropriately – often stray perilously close to comical absurdity.

Even if you manage to avoid your descriptions of fantastic settings taking on an accidental hint of comedy you will still need to stress the fact that your fantastic trees are significantly unlike familiar trees, and that all the other features of the local geography are in some way distinctive. One effect of this will be to multiply the number of adjectives used in association with every noun, pushing the style of your descriptions in the direction of 'purple prose'. It is hardly surprising that the lushest of all purple prose has been produced by fantasy writers keen on extravagant description – A. Merritt being the world champion – or that writers enthusiastic to make everything in their story seem exotic and ominous often strain the resources of their thesaurus in trying to find synonyms for 'strange'.

It is easy to mock writers whose exposition is liberally strewn with words like 'eldritch' and 'uncanny' but not so easy to find better ways of adapting pre-existent words to the description of new worlds and transformed settings. It is just as easy to disdain the frequent habit which fantasy writers have of substituting uncommon words for ordinary ones – so that grass becomes 'sward' and tree-like structures become 'dendrites' – but the careful use of exotic words can help to create an 'atmosphere' of strangeness in the world within your text.

If you do invent new words in considerable quantity you will also face the problem of making them sound and look as if they belong to a set. If they are supposed to be words in an alien language then they ought to give the impression of belonging to the *same* language. It is not usually necessary to go to the lengths of creating an actual language – although Klingon seems to have taken on a life of its own beyond the scope of *Star Trek* scripts – but some knowledge of linguistics is very useful to a writer of fantastic fiction. Tolkien's interest in Old English helped him to give immense narrative authority to the hypothetical languages of Middle-Earth. If you have no such expertise you must at least try to avoid seeming stupid; the once-fashionable practice of deriving exotic words by reversing familiar ones or using easily decoded anagrams is nowadays confined to comedy. Even if you are writing comedy, it might be as well to bear in mind that the innate comic value of silly names has been somewhat devalued by the lavish deployment of such names as Zaphod Beeblebrox and Slartibartfast in *The Hitch-Hiker's Guide to the Galaxy* and its imitators.

One particularly useful resource for writers of fantasy and science fiction in search of sets of names is mythology. Many fantasies are, of course, directly based in ancient mythologies which can be thoroughly researched, producing a ready-made set of exotic names. Given that we have already instituted the practice of calling other planets after figures in mythology, and their satellites and surface features after related figures, science fiction writers have a ready-made warrant for plundering encyclopedias of mythology for sets of names which they can apply to the cities, mountains and islands of alien worlds.

A further advantage of this strategy is that names borrowed from mythology arrive already packed full of useful symbolic implication. I find that hunting through *Dr Smith's Classical Dictionary* and similar texts for re-usable names often helps to throw up motifs and connections that can be built into my plots.

Describing actions and feelings

When your characters are involved in any complex action, especially if they are entangled in hectic conflict, the principal decision you have to make is how much detail to include. A blow-by-blow description of a game or a fight may become tedious if you take several pages of description to detail a few seconds of action, although your description may seem irritatingly vague if you do not provide some analysis of the sequence of moves involved.

The artistry of constructing action sequences within your stories has as much to do with leaving things out as putting them in. Like the director of a film, you have to decide when to cut from one momentary scene to another, but you have more scope than a film director has for 'telescoping' action, using the manner of your description to adjust the temporal flow of your story. A film director can only use slow motion and speeded-up film in moderation, because they are so obviously artificial on screen, but there is no necessary connection in a story between the space taken up by a passage of description and the time elapsed therein. When exciting things are happening you can take advantage of the inherent drama of the events to describe what is happening in minute detail, but when your characters' actions are less exciting you will probably want to collapse your account of several hours' activity into a single summary paragraph.

Not all action is hectic, of course. It is as well to remember when constructing dialogues that actual face-to-face conversations are often so extravagantly spiced with gestures that more is communicated by the 'body language' than by the actual words. In everyday life much of this body language is transmitted and received subconsciously – which makes its incorporation into stories problematic – but describing the subtler actions of your characters may help you to characterise them more deftly.

It certainly helps you to provide interesting and lively descriptions if the events and actions you are describing are themselves interesting and lively. Unfortunately, it *is* possible to produce descriptions of exciting events which remain stubbornly unexciting. Avoiding 'flat' description is just as important as avoiding 'flat' dialogue, and it can usually be done by adapting the same strategies.

Like speech, action is multi-layered; what characters intend to do and what they actually accomplish may be very different. Most of the humour of silent films is generated within the awkward gap between endeavour and accomplishment – whatever Charlie Chaplin and Harold Lloyd tried to do, it always went wrong, sometimes pathetically and sometimes spectacularly. When describing action it is worth bearing in mind that what happens to your characters is likely to be the outcome of a complex sequences of tentative moves, counter-moves, hasty readjustments and so on.

As with speech, the purposive aspects of action are compounded with elements of performance. Different people have different styles of action, but all action is to some extent *display* and if you bear this in mind it will help you to use action in characterisation and to make your descriptions more enterprising.

In exactly the same way that dialogue can be interwoven with the thoughts of the viewpoint character, so action sequences can be intercut with private exclamations of alarm or glee. The 'thought-acts' associated with violent action must be accommodated to the time-frame of the action – which usually means that they have to be very brief – but they can still be useful as enlivening devices.

There are, of course, some kinds of action which are much more inti-mately associated with thoughts and feelings than others, and which pose special problems of description in consequence. The most obvious example is sexual intercourse, which has the additional problem of being hedged about with taboos, to the extent that we have no ready language with which to talk and write about sexual matters save for the terminology of clinical jargon and a rich vocabulary of obscenities. Both of these terminologies are grotesquely inappropriate to the emotional aspects of sexual experience, forcing writers in all genres to resort to all manner of metaphors and euphemisms.

Even in known-world fiction the description of erotic feelings tends to be heavily fantasised, often confused with the language of religious experience – of ecstasy, transcendence and paradise. When intense love is not being compared to religious experience it is frequently described as a kind of madness, involving obsession and abnormal behaviour. In many fantasy and science fiction stories, states of mind which could only be delusional in known-world fiction can become literal – one character may actually undergo some kind of transcendental metamorphosis, while another's feverish dreams may indeed be the result of supernatural visitation by an incubus or succubus – and this confusion of the literal and metaphorical may make it even harder for fantasy and science fiction writers to describe erotic encounters.

Describing sex between humans and supernatural beings, or between telepaths, can be awkward because perfectly ordinary acts of sexual intercourse are so often described as if they were supernatural experiences, leaving no margin for further exaggeration. On the other hand, the fact that ordinary sexual intercourse is so often dressed up with supernatural jargon lends a special 'licence of credibility' to supernaturalised love stories. Given that actual sexual experience is so liberally laden with fantasy, both deliberate and – if there is any truth at all in Freudian theory – subconscious, it is hardly surprising that fiction in which lust and love can break the boundaries of space, time and species can carry the kind of powerful conviction that is displayed in such classic erotic fantasies as Théophile Gautier's 'Clarimonde', W. H. Hudson's *Green Mansions* and Robert Nathan's *Portrait of Jennie*.

Although it is rarely necessary to invent new words in order to describe action sequences in fantasy and science fiction it is often necessary to use fairly obscure technical jargon. Even the most mundane operations performed by scientists at work require some familiarity with laboratory apparatus and its usage, and future scientists will have to be provided with apparatus and methods of working appropriate to their time. Characters in fantasy stories who use magic also require equipment with appropriate tools and rituals. Any fighting which is not hand-to-hand will require some notion of what can and cannot be done with the relevant weapons, and fighting which is hand-to-hand may involve abstruse jargon if exotic martial arts are involved.

Like artists learning to draw human figures, writers learning to subject human characters to exotic ordeals can benefit from the study of anatomy – and because writers, unlike artists, can get inside their characters, you may need a more intimate knowledge of what happens to bodies under stress. Writers employing an element of horror in their fiction may require a certain quasi-medical expertise if they are to calculate the effects of the injuries their characters sustain with sufficient accuracy, and – perhaps more importantly – describe them with maximum gut-wrenching effect.

If your characters do suffer injury or infirmity – or even if they merely inflict injuries upon others – you may find it difficult to choose between clinical and everyday terminology. The heavy use of clinical jargon tends to produce a style which seems emotionless, not because it is devoid of feeling but because the descriptions of feeling are couched in pedantically objective terms. This can exaggerate the element of horror in passages where people are getting hurt, because treating the victims in this dispassionate way adds an extra element of 'de-humanisation' to their suffering, but it is a tactic best used in moderation. At other points in your story you will want to create sympathy for the victims, and that will be difficult if all your descriptions are couched in coldly dispassionate terms.

Like conversations, action sequences become much more complicated if they involve more than two people. It is relatively easy for a writer to track the involvement of a viewpoint character with a single other person, but much harder to organise interaction between a single viewpoint character and several others. Your viewpoint character will rarely need to function as an observer of conversations involving more than a handful of people, but may often have to function as an observer of events involving dozens, or even hundreds.

Describing large-scale events like disasters and battles poses special difficulties, although the burden can usually be reduced by sharing it between several different viewpoints. Each viewpoint can provide a part of a much bigger picture and cutting between the viewpoints helps to sustain the pace of the narrative. The kind of description you provide will depend, in large measure, on the proximity of your characters to the action. If they are in the thick of it, the narrative will have to concentrate on their particular involvement and the bigger picture will be rather vague. If you want to describe the tactics and strategy of a battle in more detail you will probably need to deploy a remote observer who can overlook the entire scene without being distracted by immediate threats.

Exposition and explanation

There are various ways in which you can use exposition to import background information into your story. This is useful because the device of having a wise old man impart vital knowledge to an innocent abroad has its limitations. If the world within your text is significantly different from the known world, you will need to drip-feed information about its differences at a relatively steady pace from the very first paragraph, leaking significant items into every passing observation your viewpoint characters make.

This kind of drip-feeding can only build a picture by slow degrees, and many of the items of information you let fall in this way will initially seem puzzling to the reader, only 'falling into place' when they have combined with other items. There will undoubtedly be times when you have to get information across to your reader in a more forthright and more concentrated fashion.

The most direct method of doing this is to employ 'texts-within-texts'. Some of the most famous fantasy and science fiction novels use the brutal device of prefacing chapters with introductory headquotes from imaginary reference books. Isaac Asimov's *Foundation* uses quotes from the *Encyclopedia Galactica*, while Frank Herbert's *Dune* uses various quasi-scriptural writings of the Princess Irulan as well as bracketing the entire text with a glossary, a map and four appendices. J. R. R. Tolkien's *The Lord of the Rings* has twenty pages of prefatory exposition and more than a hundred pages of appendices, in addition to large fold-out maps. Despite these august precedents, however, most editors will discourage writers from making extravagant use of such devices as headquotes and appendices – although they might well demand a map if you have not seen fit to provide one.

Your characters can, of course, do research of their own, and it is entirely plausible that they should, once they know that they are facing the challenge of the unknown. It is usually more economical, however, if the characters discover notes or journals made by someone else who has already done the relevant research, or receive letters summarising the results of such research. As with explanations provided by wise old men, it is often sensible to make sure that the central character's discovery of the vital document is tantalisingly delayed, so that the reader will be avid to receive the intelligence it contains.

If your viewpoint character already knows a great deal about the world within the text – and it would be absurd to work *exclusively* with innocents abroad – then they can and must convey some of that knowledge to the reader. This can be difficult to orchestrate, because you will not want your characters to be delivering what are, in effect, long explanatory lectures every time they happen to notice some detail of their world which requires explanation. You must balance the priority of informing your readers about the world within your text against the necessity of making the stream of your character's consciousness plausible. Every time your characters notice something which has changed, however, they can plausibly reflect on the reason for the change, and every time they meet other characters with particular special interests they can plausibly comment on the oddity of those interests. Even people thoroughly acquainted with the world in which they live can and do stand aside occasionally to look at it with a fresh eye and wonder at the strangeness of it.

It is as well to bear in mind when planning your texts-within-texts and explanatory reveries that what the reader and the character need to know is sometimes far less detailed than what you needed to find out in order to construct the story. It is easy for writers to become over-enthusiastic about passing on the rewards of their own research to the reader, perhaps feeling that they have been wasting their time unless they can make full use of their own research notes. You must beware of burdening your reader with information that the story does not require.

Some writers like to know a great deal more about the worlds within their texts than they will ever tell their readers. Some like to keep elaborate dossiers on their characters, highly detailed maps of imaginary territory, plans of fictitious buildings, extensive chronologies of events and so on. If you are working on a long story you will probably find it necessary to do *some* work of this sort in order to make sure that you do not contradict yourself. You should always remember, though, that the function of such aids is to provide your story with sturdy foundations; not only is there no necessity to transfer all the data into the story itself but you must actively resist the temptation to do so. Even if the reader will need to know most of it, the form in which it is best delivered to the reader is likely to be much more economical than the form in which it is most useful to you.

Having said all this, however, it is worth remembering that at least some readers do appreciate being told a good deal about the worlds within their favourite texts. Readers, like writers, can become obsessed with fictitious worlds to the extent that they want to cultivate an intimate acquaintance with them. These readers, at least, will be more than willing to take on board the substance of massive and blatant info-dumps – to the extent that there is a small but substantial market for 'concordances' and other supplementary texts which process all the available information about the best-known imaginary worlds into reference book form. Examples include *The Dune Encyclopedia* and *Lexicon Urthus* (a companion to Gene Wolfe's 'New Sun' series).

Whatever writing manuals may say about the desperate necessity of avoiding indigestible info-dumps, the fact remains that truly interesting worlds within texts do demand a great deal of imaginative labour on the part of writer and reader alike. If such worlds are to work as well as they can they really do require the kinds of elaborate invention that can only be conveyed in lists and glossaries, histories and sociological analyses. Deciding where to put such extravagant info-dumps is never easy, but if you decide never to do it at all you will restrict yourself to working with imaginary worlds which are very similar to our own and never fully realised.

7

BEYOND THE SLUSH PILE: MARKETING FANTASY AND SCIENCE FICTION

Manuscript preparation

Your submission manuscripts must be double-spaced, alternating lines of type with blank lines. Leave margins at least an inch wide all around the text. These measures ensure that there is adequate space for copy editors to mark up the typescript.

Each page of your manuscript should be numbered and each page number should be accompanied by an identifier of some sort that will tell an editor which typescript a mislaid page belongs to. I use a header which includes both my name and the story title.

If you are using a word processor do not 'right justify' your text. Straightening up the right-hand edge of the text makes it more difficult for editors to read, and to judge whether you have unintentionally left two spaces between words.

When presenting a script it is not important to imitate the finished style of a printed book. You should aim simply to supply a print out that is easy to follow. This applies to paragraph layout in particular. You may not know whether the design style indents new paragraphs or leaves space between them. Just keep your presentation simple and the book designer will sort this out for you.

Where you want the typesetter to leave a blank line in the set text, you should emphasise the blank line by putting in a few asterisks (otherwise the text break might get lost at the end of a page).

Underline words that you want to be set in italics. If you put them in italics yourself using the "italic" function on a word processor, it makes it harder for the copy editor to pick them out. Such formatting may be lost if your typescript is saved on disk in a different program from that of the publisher.

The first page of your manuscript should contain its title, your by-line (followed by your real name if the by-line is a pseudonym), your address and an approximate word count. Don't worry too much about the word count; editors will usually make their own anyhow. Editors want to know how much space a story will take up rather than the actual number of words in it but there is more than one conventional way of rendering this measure as a 'word count'; a count of actual words is usually near enough but if your story has a lot of short paragraphs and other stretching effects you might want to increase the total by ten per cent or so to take that into account.

It is usually a bad idea to use different fonts within your story. Courier is becoming established as the 'standard' font for typescripts prepared by word processor. Pitch 10 is preferable on the grounds of readability but I use pitch 12 because it saves paper – the difference is significant because most of my markets are in the United States and international postage is so expensive. Remember that on word processors, the higher the figure the larger the font size.

Do not bind your manuscript. There is a slight conflict of interest with regard to methods of holding the pages together. You want to make sure that your manuscript stays in one piece but many editors prefer to read loose sheets. Some editors dislike staples while others hate paper clips, so there is no ideal solution to the problem, although novel-length manuscripts can be safely secured with a rubber band. I use a single, easily removable staple on manuscripts up to 30 pages, a small bulldog clip on manuscripts between 30 and 90 pages, and rubber bands on anything larger.

Submission

Always make it as easy as possible for editors to respond to your submissions. Always include adequate return postage. If you want your manuscript back you must attach sufficient postage to a self-addressed envelope of an appropriate size. If not, include some clear indication that the manuscript is a photocopy that may be thrown away and include a self-addressed envelope with sufficient postage to carry a one-page reply.

If you are making international submissions you can include International Reply Coupons instead of attaching stamps to your self-addressed envelope but this is more expensive than obtaining stamps from the country to which you are submitting. Because the American short story market is so much bigger than the domestic market I find it convenient to keep a substantial supply of US stamps. All my submissions to the USA are disposable photocopies, each accompanied by a self-addressed air-mail envelope with sixty cents worth of stamps on it; all my UK submissions include a large envelope with sufficient stamps to cover the return of the manuscript.

Your covering letter should be simple and formal. For US submission I use a standard template which reads:

> Dear [editor's name]
>
> I enclose a story called [story title] which you might care to consider for [magazine name]. The manuscript is a photocopy and need not be returned; I enclose a stamped self-addressed envelope for your reply.
>
> Yours sincerely
>
> [space for signature]
>
> Brian Stableford

If I have met the editor or have previously received a personal letter of some kind (a letter of acceptance qualifies), then I use a first name in the salutation and sign the letter with my own given name; if not, I use the editor's title and surname and sign my full name.

Many inexperienced writers are tempted to embroider this process by packaging their typescript in fancy ways or including an extravagant advertisement for their story in their covering letter. Such tactics are unwise; they never help and may well be annoying. Remember that every submission you make is part of an ongoing campaign; ideally, the package you send out should give the impression that you are a competent professional whose work is worthy of serious consideration. At the very least, you must make sure that you do not give the impression that you are an attention-seeking time-waster.

When submitting short stories you should always send the complete text. You may, however, submit novels in the form of an outline and a few sample chapters. Many editors prefer to see outlines and samples because it saves them time in identifying items in which they are definitely not interested, and some like to have an outline in addition to a full text because reading the outline may well save them the bother of looking at the text.

A novel outline should be as concise as possible. It should be a summary, not an overt advertisement, although it is permissible to call attention to any 'unique selling points' the work might have. My outlines for novels and novel series tend to be three or four pages long. A few introductory paragraphs identify the sub-genre to which the work belongs, its anticipated length, the setting and the main characters; these are followed by a rough sketch of the plot, then by an estimate of the time I would require to complete the project. Forty pages of sample text should be enough to allow an editor to decide whether there would be any point in looking at the full text.

The politics of submission

The most vexing problem faced by writers who are just starting out is the time taken up by the submission process. There is no way around this. Typescripts from unknown writers are automatically diverted into 'slush piles' by the editors to whom they are submitted. Slush piles accumulate so rapidly, and contain such a high percentage of unsuitable material, that almost all editors use outside readers to go through them and pick out the rare items that may be worth the editor's personal attention. The whole process usually takes several months.

To make a bad situation even worse, stories which do sell can remain in a magazine's inventory for anything between three months and three years before they actually get into print.

Inexperienced writers, frustrated by the endless waiting, are sometimes tempted to speed things up by submitting a story to several different markets simultaneously. *You must not do this.* Editors need to know that the stories they read are available to them should they wish to buy them; if they make an offer for a story only to be told that it has already been sold elsewhere they become extremely annoyed.

Inexperienced writers who build up a backlog of unsold manuscripts are sometimes tempted to send them out in batches, but this creates a bad impression. There is no reason why you should not have two or three stories submitted at reasonable intervals patiently making their way to the top of a particular slush pile but sending out batches is tantamount to an admission that the items in question are rejects from elsewhere.

The only way to speed up the submission process is to avoid the slush pile and get your manuscripts into the privileged pile to which the editor intends to give personal attention. The usual way to accomplish this is to sell a story to the magazine in question; editors who have already published you will at least ask their readers to give priority to your typescript. Some writers try to take advantage of the fact that they have sold a story *somewhere* by mentioning it in the covering letters they send to other editors; some even take advantage of the opportunities offered by word processing to maintain a constantly updated list of publications which they include, along with their covering letters, with all their submissions. This probably does no harm, provided that the relevance of the information outweighs the suggestion of desperation.

It is worth bearing in mind that there are other ways to familiarise editors with your name. Polite letters of comment on the contents of the magazine might help to prepare the way for future submissions. If the magazine to which you would like to submit work carries book reviews by various hands you might find an opening there. Some hopeful writers habitually seek out more famous writers and interview them, in order that they may use well-known names as a launching-pad for their own by-line. Those who live close to editors or their offices can volunteer to help out by reading their slush piles. None of these ventures is likely to be lucrative in itself, but all may serve to generate good will. In the final analysis, however, the only way to obtain favourable consideration from editors is to demonstrate that your work is always worth looking at – and the only way to do this is to publish on a regular basis.

The more work you sell, the easier it becomes to get a rapid response to further submissions. Unfortunately, 'rapid' can still mean several weeks, and the weeks can still stretch into months. No matter how good your standing becomes, some submissions will always seem to have vanished into a black hole. A polite letter requesting a response may be appropriate eventually, but you ought to wait for at least three months after the submission date. I send such enquiries if an editor with whom I deal regularly has taken twice as long as usual to respond. If I have not had a response after a year, I generally send a brief letter saying that in the absence of a reply I assume that the story is unwanted and that I intend to submit it elsewhere.

The submission process is even slower where novels are concerned. Slush piles of novels are more difficult to whittle down than slush piles of short stories and often get completely out of hand. Publishers will usually read submissions from literary agents much more quickly than unsolicited manuscripts, but agents have their slush piles too and an unpublished writer may find the process of acquiring an agent to be just as awkward as the process of direct submission to publishers.

Few agents nowadays will handle short fiction so you will have to handle magazine submissions yourself, but you may find it useful to submit novels via an agent if you can persuade one to act on your behalf. The real value of agents, however, lies in their ability to negotiate contracts on terms that are slightly more favourable to an author than the author will otherwise be offered, and in their ability to handle foreign rights. Most agents are part of a worldwide network which makes it easy for them to send copies of your published work to agencies in several other countries. Most British agents will work with a US 'partner' and translation rights – especially French and German translation rights – can be a very valuable addition to a writer's income.

With novels, as with short stories, the only way to speed up the submission process is to give an agent or a publisher good grounds to think that it might be worth paying prompt attention to your work – and the best way to do that is to build up an impressive 'track record'. When submitting your first novel it is definitely useful to have a long list of previous publications in magazines, and you should certainly show such a list to an agent if you want to be taken on as a client.

Inexperienced writers often find it very hard to accept that they have no automatic entitlement to publication. It simply is not true that 'if you're good enough, they have to publish you'. The sad fact is that an editor is perfectly entitled to reject your submission on any grounds whatsoever. Stories which are perfectly publishable may still require three or four submissions before they sell; stories of mine have occasionally clocked up ten rejections before eventually selling. It is perilously easy to feel that the editor who has just rejected your latest masterpiece is a criminal idiot who ought to be hung, drawn and quartered, but you will save yourself a lot of heartache if you can learn to take such misfortunes in your stride.

Because your work is a form of self-expression it is extremely difficult to accept that rejection is not personal, but if you cannot learn to forgive editors who reject your work you must at least learn to turn the other cheek. If all you get is a printed rejection slip, try to understand that all editors must work under tremendous pressure of time. If the editor writes you a letter telling you why your submission is being rejected the intention is not to hurt you but to help you – and no matter how bad the adverse comments make you feel you must try not only to take the criticisms seriously but also to be grateful for the trouble the editor has taken in making them. Next time you submit work to an editor who has written a personal note along with a rejection, offer your thanks with as much sincerity as you can muster. Writers who berate editors for failing to buy their work are fools, even if they are geniuses too.

One conclusion to be drawn from this list of evil circumstances is that you cannot afford to wait for a response to one submission before moving on to the next. You have to maintain your production in the absence of any substantial feedback, and even in the face of a steady stream of rejections. No writer ever gets to like receiving rejection slips, just as no boxer ever gets to like being hit in the face, but it is something you have to learn to tolerate if you intend to stay in the game. If you can maintain your motivation in the face of continual rejection, or use rejection as a spur to make yourself try harder, you *will* eventually succeed.

Finding markets

The literary marketplace may be roughly divided into 'mass-market' outlets and 'small presses'. In Britain there are two annual guides to mass market magazines and publishers: *The Writers' and Artists' Yearbook* and *The Writers' Directory*. Both can be obtained from any sizeable bookshop and both are useful, all the more so because of the articles they publish alongside the market lists on such matters as copyright law and copy-editing practice. They also contain lists of agents, with notes of their specialisms, and lists of organisations of interest to writers.

Small press magazines often have very short lifespans, and small press publishers have a far more precarious existence than mass-market publishers (many of which are part of larger commercial conglomerates). For this reason they are much harder to keep track of, and the standard guide books are far less efficient in recording them than they are in recording mass-market outlets. There is, however, a specialised *Small Press Guide* published by the Writers' Bookshop; this is less likely to be available in high street bookshops but can be obtained by mail order from 7–11 Kensington High Street, London W8 5NP.

Although fantasy and science fiction publications are listed in these general guides you will undoubtedly find it useful to have access to specialist market reports. The *Bulletin* of the Science-Fiction and Fantasy Writers of America publishes regularly updated market reports but you have to be a published writer to qualify for membership of the organisation. The best generally available printed source of specialist market information is *Science Fiction Chronicle*, which updates its account of the US market every six months or so and publishes a supplement on the UK market about once a year. The magazine's address is PO Box 022730, Brooklyn, New York, NY 11202-3308, USA but UK subscriptions (currently £29 for a year, £55 for two years) can be obtained from Rob Hansen, 144 Plashet Grove, London E6 1AB.

People with access to the Internet can find continually updated market reports at: http://www.sff.net/people/Julia.West/markets.html

Occasional market reports appear in *Locus*, a monthly magazine which is effectively the 'trade journal' of the science fiction and fantasy fields. *Locus* offers by far the best overview of the field, including comprehensive lists of publications and forthcoming publications, excellent book and magazine reviews, and an annual 'review' which includes data on the economic fortunes of all the leading magazines. No one with a serious professional interest in the field can afford to be without it; its address is PO Box 13305, Oakland, California, CA 94661, USA but UK subscriptions (currently $48 per year surface mail, $70 per year airmail) can be obtained from Fantast (Medway) Ltd, PO Box 23, Upwell, Wisbech, Cambridgeshire, PE14 9BU.

Occasional UK market reports can be found in *Matrix*, the bimonthly newsletter of the British Science Fiction Association. The BSFA also publishes an occasional periodical for would-be writers called *Focus* and runs a number of postal writers' workshops called 'orbiters'. Membership of the BSFA currently costs £18 per year (£12 for the unwaged), available from 1 Long Row Close, Everdon, Daventry, Northamptonshire NN11 3BE. There is also a British Fantasy Society which publishes a bimonthly newsletter; membership of the BFS is £17 per year, available from 2 Harwood Street, Stockport SK4 1JJ.

At present the UK has only one mass-market magazine that publishes science fiction and fantasy. This is *Interzone*, whose editorial address in 217 Preston Drove, Brighton BN1 6FL. All Britons interested in writing short fiction within the field ought to familiarise themselves with the magazine, which has extensive review columns that monitor relevant UK publications and a page of small ads where small press magazines are frequently advertised. *Interzone* is available in most larger branches of W. H. Smith's but subscriptions can be obtained from the editorial address at £32 per year (twelve issues).

Australia's longest-established genre market is *Aurealis*, published twice-yearly by Chimaera Publications, PO Box 2164, Mount Waverley, Victoria 3149, and Canada's is *On Spec*, published quarterly by The Copper Pig Collective, Box 4727, Edmonton, Alberta, T6E 5G6. The extent to which America dominates the genre market place is clearly evident in the fact that the USA has ten times as many outlets as the rest of the English speaking world.

The rates of pay obtainable for fantasy and science fiction stories vary enormously. It is possible to receive payment of over a thousand dollars from a few select outlets in the USA but the great majority of mass-market outlets there pay between five and eight cents per word. Small press outlets may pay anywhere between five cents a word and nothing at all but most market reports ignore non-paying publications and often describe those paying less than two cents a word as 'semi-professional'. *Interzone* pays £30 per thousand words.

The advances obtainable for novels are equally variable. Mass-market publishers in the USA will usually offer between $1,000 and $5,000 for a first novel, although $10,000 may be achievable if the novel has some selling point which is out of the ordinary. In the UK a writer might expect to get £1,000 or £2,000 for a first novel, although £5,000 might be obtained for a novel with unusual sales potential. Established writers well-known to the readers would expect to get $10,000 in the USA or £5,000 in the UK as a matter of course, and would certainly expect more for a book with more than usual market appeal.

A book which sells well might earn additional royalties over and above these advances, but this is unlikely and if it does happen you will not see the money until several years have passed. On the other hand, a book which sells very well will allow you to demand a bigger advance next time out and may even start rival publishers bidding for your services. In the rarefied heights of the marketplace occupied by best-sellers, advances in hundreds of thousands of pounds or millions of dollars are nowadays routinely paid out – but only a dozen or so fantasy and science fiction writers have so far attained that goal. There used to be a middle range spanning the market from bottom to top, but that part of the spectrum has faded out in recent times; nowadays a select few full-time writers earn enormous amounts of money while the rest make do with relatively modest returns.

For obvious reasons, the more a market pays the harder it is to break into. Some writers are disdainful of small presses – especially of the ones that pay nothing at all – but they offer a very useful training ground. The mass market does not select purely in terms of quality; there are some kinds of fantastic fiction – short horror fiction and 'antiquarian fantasy' are the most obvious – which are almost entirely confined to the world of small presses, and writers interested in these sub-genres may have to be content with very low rates of pay no matter how good they are.

The quality of small press magazines varies also but the best of them (especially the best American examples) are produced with loving care and some are far more attractive in appearance than mass-market magazines whose priorities are purely commercial. Personally, I am quite happy to give away that fraction of my output which falls outside the scope of the mass-market magazines and am always proud to appear in the magazines to which I donate it. It is possible for writers to build up a considerable literary reputation based on small press publications and such outlets can be very useful in nurturing writers through the early phases of their careers.

The requirements of different markets vary considerably, and it is always wise to check the specific requirements of a publication carefully before submitting to it. The process of submission takes long enough without wasting effort in submissions that cannot possibly succeed.

Most mass-market fantasy and science fiction magazines are not much interested in stories less than 2,000 words long but the competition for the available space gets much fiercer if stories are longer than 6,000 words. There is no point in savagely abridging a story whose natural length is far above that, but if you can produce stories which can comfortably be confined by those two word-limits you will find abundant opportunities to publish them. Unfortunately, the work

involved in establishing exotic worlds within texts makes it frustratingly difficult to produce fantasy and science fiction stories as short as
6,000 words.

The politics of production

Writers work in many different ways, according to their personalities,
but the key to productivity is tenacity. The biggest problem facing
writers whose writing does not provide an income, or whose writing
income is inadequate to support them, is finding the time to write. If
you are serious about writing it is essential for you to make time, and
to make time *on a regular basis*. As long as you can set a target and
keep on getting near it, the work will materialise – but as soon as you
let the target slip too far you risk production being permanently
stalled.

Many people find it impossible to imagine that full-time writers can
be at their desks from 9 am until 12.30 pm and from 1.30 pm until
5 pm, five days a week, fifty weeks a year. This is partly because they
are sceptical about the ability of people who are not bound by contrac-
tual working hours to discipline themselves and partly because they
find it difficult to believe that writers can simply sit down and switch
on their creativity at will. They are, of course, absolutely right to be
sceptical on both counts.

I do actually try to work something resembling a normal working day,
between three and four hours in the morning and again in the after-
noon, five days a week, but it would be hypocritical to pretend that I
always compensate for any time that I might lose. Some writers fix a
daily target of words or pages but I find that a little too limiting; I
prefer to make week-by-week schedules according to the nature of the
work I have in hand. I compose non-fiction much more slowly than
fiction, but once I have composed it subsequent revisions are rarely
more than mere tinkering. I am much more slapdash in composing
fiction, and often have to revise chapters very extensively, weeks or
months after they were first drafted, and I sometimes have to revise
them several times over.

My schedules are always being torn down and rewritten, but each one is an aim rather than a compulsion. I rarely meet their calculatedly overdemanding requirements but if I couldn't get reasonably close I couldn't function as a professional writer. You may have far less time available but you have to function in much the same way. Even if you can only make thirty minutes a day available for writing you must try to preserve that thirty minutes and you must do everything you can to make sure that you actually fill it up by *writing*. It is worth bearing in mind that even if you can produce no more than one page a day five days a week you can still finish a novel in a year or eighteen months, provided that you write *every day*.

The problem of switching on your creativity whenever you sit down to write is probably more acute than the problem of making time. Rumour has it that there are writers who can switch their creativity on and off as if they were turning a tap and never have to revise a word, but if they really do exist they are very rare birds indeed. Sometimes, I find writing very slow work; sometimes, what I write is utter drivel. Unless you are very lucky, the same will be true for you – but you have to keep going regardless.

I try my best to keep plugging on even when production is sluggish and when I am uncomfortably aware that I am writing rubbish – after all, slow production is better than no production and there is usually something salvageable in a mountain of dross – but it can be very difficult. Occasionally, my head begins to ache in protest and I have to give up, but not without a fight. You will doubtless find that there are times when you really *cannot* do it, but you ought to try as hard as you can. Waiting for inspiration is like waiting for a bus in a blizzard: it's always late and sometimes never arrives at all.

Writing is a solitary occupation, and a writer's struggles are essentially internal. No one can help you while you are wrestling with the almost-irresistible urge to give up and do something else instead. It may, however, help you to know that there are other people who routinely face similar predicaments, and with whom you can compare notes. Writers can and do communicate with one another, often forming loose communities, and you might well derive considerable moral support from communication with others like yourself.

The extra-mural departments of many universities and colleges offer evening classes in 'Creative Writing', at least some of which provide opportunities for participants to submit work for 'workshop' discussion. (I do an annual ten-week evening course on 'Writing Fiction' for the University of Reading.) The various regions of Britain all have local Arts Associations partly funded by the Arts Council and these Arts Associations can usually supply information on creative writing courses and other writers' groups. They sometimes arrange short courses of their own and many of them also have their own small press publications.

The Australia Council has a Literature Board which provides subsidies to a wide range of publications and administers grants directly to writers. The USA has a wide range of institutions that provide grants to writers and publishers, and almost all American universities offer full-credit courses in Creative Writing.

Science fiction and fantasy readers are much more inclined to communicate with one another than fans of other genres, and this is one of the reasons why science fiction and fantasy are so strongly represented in the world of small presses. Because writers in these genres are frequently recruited from the ranks of habitual readers there are sizeable contingents of writers at most science fiction conventions and some writers who live close to one another habitually attend monthly gatherings. Would-be writers may find it useful to infiltrate such institutions, where useful information about markets can often be gleaned; the British Science Fiction Association and the British Fantasy Society are useful sources of information about local sf groups and their newsletters publish up-to-date lists of impending conventions.

Pleasing the audience

It is as well to remember that not all readers are alike. The greatest writer who ever lived could not please all of the people all of the time. In fact, the greatest writer who ever lived could not even please all of the people some of the time or some of the people all of the time. The best you can hope for is to please some of the people some of the time.

There are many writers who want to please as many people as possible. There are many, too, who would rather please the few than the many, always provided that they are the right few.

There is nothing paradoxical in the fact that writers who set out to please as many people as possible usually fail to please the few who have fixed and elaborate opinions as to how writing should best be done. Given that tastes vary, it is highly likely that writing which is geared to please a wide range of tastes will lack the piquancy necessary to win the wholehearted approval of tightly focused tastes.

Different readers have very different opinions about the ways in which writers ought to exercise their creative power. Anyone ambitious to write fantasy and science fiction will know already that there are some readers who do not like anything to happen within the world of a text that could not happen in the real world. Some commentators on literature consider realistic texts to be intrinsically more worthwhile than fantastic ones, often because they think that although such texts might be useful for relaxation – because they are inherently 'escapist' – they cannot possibly be as *serious* as texts which represent life as it really could be lived, whose characters face problems and dilemmas which readers might actually have to face themselves. This is, however, not something which should worry a writer of fantasy or science fiction. Even if such judgments were sound they would be narrow-minded, and they are probably misled. After all, a marked preference for realistic fiction is a recent fad. If Homer, Shakespeare and Dickens were happy to write fantasies, why should you and I feel the least hint of embarrassment about it?

There are, of course, other readers who overturn the preferences of those who equate 'realistic' with 'serious'. Some readers find texts which contain worlds identical to their own boring, or even oppressive in their insistence that the way things are is the only way they could be. There are also some readers who find realistic texts interesting enough within their self-imposed limits but think that such texts can never attain the sublime heights of achievement open to texts whose worlds are so much grander and more glorious than the world of everyday existence. You are free to aim your work at any kind of reader you like, or as many kinds as you might hope to attract.

Given that you have picked up this book you are more likely to look kindly upon the production of texts whose worlds are out of the ordinary than people who have turned away from it, but you might still hold opinions which are quite different from its other readers. Among those who do not disapprove of 'non-realistic' texts there are many smaller parties, some of which are fervently opposed to one another. Some fantasy readers don't like science fiction, and some science fiction readers don't like fantasy. Some lovers of 'hard' science fiction think that much of what is labelled 'science fiction' is insufficiently rigorous, and some lovers of 'dark' fantasy think that trilogies describing heroic quests in quasi-Medieval worlds are too formulaic... and so on.

The relevance of this to you, the writer, is that it can be frustratingly difficult to figure out how to fit your stories into particular publishing categories, let alone to make them attractive to editors and readers who use those categories as guidelines. There is no single set of rules – however loosely they are framed – that can determine the effect that a particular narrative move will have on its intended audience. The propriety of such moves varies according to the particular audience involved, and may also change over time. Nor is it the case that any rule you do decide to observe cannot occasionally be broken to good effect.

It is as well for a writer contemplating the production of fantasy or science fiction stories to know something about the various populations of readers who form the marketplace for these genres, and also to bear in mind that these populations are unstable. The ultimate prize for a writer is not to fit your work perfectly to the demands of an existing audience but to conjure up a new audience where there was none before. It is, however, useful to know something about the various 'sub-genres' and 'niche markets' of fantasy and science fiction, and about their historical development.

Changing fashions in fantastic fiction

The literary marketplace is subject to rapidly changing fashions. The range of available outlets changes often and suddenly, and so does the demand for various kinds of fiction. The publishing industry is very vulnerable to booms and slumps, partly because book publishers work on a time-scale which forces them to make their plans between one and two years in advance; anything which happens in the interim – whether it be a sharp rise in paper prices or an abrupt shift in the interests of the reading public – always throws those plans into disarray. Editors live an anxious existence, always desperate not to miss out on the latest fad, and they tend to follow success like flocks of sheep; one thing you can always be sure of is that today's biggest best-seller will generate a host of copycat exercises two years down the line, many of which will sink without trace.

For these reasons, any account of the present state of the marketplace for fantastic fiction is likely to go out of date very rapidly. All I can reasonably attempt to do is to offer some observations about the evolution of the marketplace in the recent past and the major trends that are currently observable.

The most remarkable phenomenon in the recent history of publishing was the establishment of 'fantasy' as a category label, which happened as a direct result of the entirely unexpected success of the American paperback editions of J. R. R. Tolkien's *The Lord of the Rings*. Until those paperback editions were released in the late 1960s, fantasy was considered to be commercially insignificant, save as a category of children's fiction. The assumption made by publishers and critics was that the imaginative legacy of myth and folklore – wizards, elves, dragons, and so on – had been 'worn out'. Children were deemed to be capable of the 'suspension of belief' required to participate in such stories, by virtue of their relative innocence, but adults were supposed to consider them unworthy of consideration. The few fantasy paperbacks that were aimed at an adult audience – most of them 'sword and sorcery' novels or comic fantasies reprinted from American pulp magazines of the 1930s and 1940s – were released as part of science fiction lines, often carrying the science fiction label.

The success of Tolkien's trilogy – which was recently voted the most significant work of the twentieth century in a poll organised by Waterstone's bookshops – demonstrated to publishers that they themselves had fallen victim to a myth. Contemporary adults are, indeed, capable of the 'suspension of disbelief' required to participate wholeheartedly in a tale of wizards, elves and countless other imaginary beings, and they are willing to buy such works in quantity. Since 1970, therefore, a steadily increasing fraction of the space given over to science fiction and fantasy in bookshops has been taken up by heroic fantasy, and publishers which had formerly sheltered a few fugitive fantasies under the science fiction label have gradually given more and more slots over to explicitly labelled fantasy.

Another myth widely believed by editors until the 1980s was that humorous fantasy and science fiction did not sell. That too was proved false by the enormous success of writers like Douglas Adams, Piers Anthony and Terry Pratchett. Terry Pratchett is currently the best-selling fantasy author in the UK and his success has helped to open market space for other writers of humorous fantasy, but comedy is much harder to formularise and imitate than earnest action-adventure fiction, so there are far more Robert E. Howard clones and Tolkien clones to be found on bookshop shelves than Pratchett clones – and the latter tend to seem horribly second-rate when compared with the original.

As far as novels are concerned, many editors would rather publish fantasies because they believe that fantasies are potentially accessible to all readers, while science fiction novels are thought to appeal to a more restricted constituency. However, the market for short stories is much more heavily biased towards science fiction, partly because the long-established science fiction magazines have an established population of loyal subscribers and partly because the kinds of fantasy which sell best are the ones which require stories of considerable length (usually several volumes).

One consequence of this state of affairs is that it is easier to 'serve an apprenticeship' as a science fiction writer by writing short fiction for magazines, but more difficult to carry that career forward into regular book production. More and more outlets for short fantasy are opening up, however – especially in the small press arena – and fantasy writers may find it easier in future to build up a track record in short fiction. Although short 'dark fantasies' and supernatural horror stories are almost entirely confined to small press outlets such publications often have a strong and enthusiastic following. This is a problematic area in that writers can sometimes build a considerable reputation while finding it extremely difficult to earn any significant amount of money, at least until they graduate to writing novels.

The increasing popularity of fantasy has had a marked effect on the kinds of science fiction that editors are enthusiastic to buy. It has always been the case that a good deal of action/adventure science fiction is distinguishable from fantasy only in terms of its jargon, and many editors within the field feel that the only way that science fiction can duplicate the popularity of fantasy is to imitate it as closely as possible.

One result of this is that the 'hard' science fiction – science fiction that attempts to be rigorous in its scientific extrapolations – which once seemed to provide the 'core' of the genre is now rather peripheral, at least in marketing terms. The marginalisation of hard science fiction has been assisted by two other trends which have become very marked in recent years: the influence of the visual media and the changing constituency of the readers in terms of balance of the sexes.

The success of such TV shows as *Star Trek* and *The X-Files* and such films as *Star Wars* and *Alien* has caused a dramatic increase in the importance of science fiction in the visual media. Because TV shows and films in general attract a much bigger audience than books the economic base of the science fiction genre has shifted into the visual media; the science fiction books which sell best today are those which are tied in to TV shows and films. The kinds of science fiction which are most easily adaptable to the visual media are, of course, space-set action/adventure stories which make abundant use of models and computer-generated special effects and sf/horror stories which use known-world settings. Although genre fantasy has not made such spectacular progress in the visual media, partly because it poses different and more challenging problems for special effects technicians, the type of science fiction that thrives in the visual media is mostly fantasy in hi-tech disguise.

The 1970s saw a dramatic influx of female writers into the science fiction field, and an equally dramatic influx of female readers. This had something to do with the inherent appeal of speculative fiction to feminist writers, who could employ sf as a medium for exploring the possibilities of women's liberation. Certainly, science fiction studies, especially in American universities, were taken up enthusiastically by large numbers of feminist critics. However, the most obvious shift in the popular marketplace was not towards feminist science fiction but femin*ised* science fiction of a kind more akin to genre romance. Recent science fiction has therefore become gradually less concerned with hi-tech hardware and more concerned with the personal problems of its characters.

In blatant defiance of this general trend, the most recent sub-genre of science fiction to attain a special fashionability was 'cyberpunk' fiction, which was popularised by the enormous success in the mid-1980s of William Gibson's *Neuromancer*. This was the novel that first made extravagant use of the 'cyberspace' of the world's computer network, imagining it as a new frontier ripe for exploration and exploitation by soldiers of fortune. The success of the novel was partly due to the fact that it provided computer enthusiasts with a vocabulary, a mythology and a mystique; Gibson and fellow writers Bruce Sterling and Rudy Rucker became gurus of a new sub-culture anchored by such 'new edge' magazines as *Mondo 2000* and *Wired*.

The newness of this vogue was largely an effect of the fact that previous science fiction had failed dismally to foresee the course of the computer revolution. It is now impossible to put forward any plausible vision of the near future which does not give a central role to information technology (IT) and to the network formed by the world's media and communications systems. One result of this necessity is, however, that cyberspace has been so completely 'domesticated' that it no longer seems like an untracked wilderness or an untamed frontier. The rapid evolution of information technology still offers abundant scope for the ingenious exercise of the science-fictional imagination – especially if IT evolution is interactively coupled with other revolutionary technologies like nanotechnology and genetic engineering – but writers who intend to work in this area need to keep their fingers firmly on the pulse of real-world developments because this kind of fiction dates as rapidly as real computers do.

Another recent trend in fantastic fiction has been the revitalisation of horror fiction, although there seems to be a much wider gulf separating such best-selling writers as Stephen King, Dean R. Koontz, Clive Barker and R. L. Stine from the 'second division writers' than there is in heroic fantasy or science fiction. Those publishers who have tried to develop horror lists have usually found it difficult; as with humorous fantasy the success of a few particular authors does not seem to have boosted demand for the sub-genre as a whole. The horror market is very volatile and writers interested in the field need to pay particular attention to the fast-changing small press market, where almost all the outlets for short horror fiction are located.

Like science fiction, horror has been spectacularly successful in the visual media by virtue of the rapid sophistication of cinematic special effects, but that success has had a very patchy effect on the fortunes of horror books. One very noticeable effect, however, has been the rapid growth of fiction which uses science-fictional ideas to horrific effect. Aliens – which had largely shed their horrific connotations in the anti-xenophobic 1906s – are again being commonly featured as loathsome figures of menace, and the end of the Cold War seems to have shifted the focus of social anxieties away from rival political systems towards the shadowy realm of the 'paranormal'. If you are interested in exploiting that kind of paranoia, however, you might be be wise to couch your work as non-fiction rather than fiction.

Some notes in conclusion

A careful study of the shape of the marketplace for fantasy and science fiction will certainly help you to find the markets likely to be most hospitable to your work. Reading as widely as possible within the field will also help you to get a feel for contemporary trends and may supply you with lots of ideas that you can modify to suit your own purposes. It is worth remembering, however, that one of the most valuable and interesting aspects of fantastic fiction is that it accommodates the weirdest and most wonderful literary adventures of all. The literary works which break the boundaries most comprehensively and most spectacularly are often written by people who had no idea that the boundaries were ever there.

If your principal interest in teaching yourself to write fantasy and science fiction is to make money, the lesson of the marketplace seems to be reasonably clear: write feminised trilogies in the mould established by Tolkien. That is the kind of work which is relatively easy to fake and is likely to sell fairly well, even if it never reaches the heights of best-sellerdom achieved by the most skilful of the imitators who started before you. On the other hand, precisely because this lesson is so glaringly obvious you can be certain that the competition will be stiff. You will still need some special selling point to set your work apart from the rest, and it may be harder to figure out how to make a small but crucial change in a well-established formula than to do something completely different. The greatest rewards of all will always go to the writer who sets the *next* standard for imitation – although history informs us that many fantasists who did set new standards did not survive long enough to enjoy, or even to witness, the full extent of their success.

If your principal interest in teaching yourself to write fantasy and science fiction is to produce work which will be uniquely, recognisably and definitively *yours* – irrespective of whether you can get a living wage out of it – you may have to search long and hard for suitable outlets. Many fine writers of highly original fantastic fiction had to be content with a single sympathetic editor and more than a few had to become their own editors in order to secure sympathy where none could otherwise be found. There is, however, such a deep satisfaction to be gained from publishing work which is uniquely yours – work which no one else would have or could have done – that you might justifiably consider it to be worth all the effort required.

Hopefully, this book will have offered some assistance to you whatever your particular interest might be.

GLOSSARY OF SPECIALISED TERMS

alternative history

A story which presents an image of the world as it might have become had some crucial event in history worked out differently. The conventional jargon term used in science fiction circles is the grammatically dubious 'alternate history', although historians who take the game very seriously seem to prefer 'counterfactual history'.

concealed environment stories

Stories set in worlds which seem exotic until revealed (usually in a feeble punch-line) to be something rather more familiar. There are also concealed identity stories in which the central character is eventually revealed (again, usually in a feeble punch-line) to be someone whose name is well-known. Far more stories of these kinds are written than ever see publication; 'Shaggy God stories' in which science fictional plots are ultimately "resolved" by reference to religious mythology are the most commonplace.

conceptual breakthrough

A moment of (usually dazzling) enlightenment which allows the characters in a science fiction story to achieve a vital progressive transformation of their world-view.

Frankenstein syndrome, The

A term coined by Isaac Asimov to refer to the tacit technophobia of the kind of science fiction story in which an new invention runs amok and has to be destroyed, often along with its creator. Such stories remain very appealing to writers, however, because they are inherently melodramatic (if the invention works according to plan there's no story!) and because it is easy to formulate climaxes and endings for them.

known-world stories

In much the same way that blind people have had to coin a term to describe people who are not blind ('sighted'), people who write about imaginative fiction need a term for fiction which does not involve sciencefictional or supernatural devices. 'Unimaginative fiction' obviously will not do, and 'mundane fiction', although widely used for this purpose, has a similarly pejorative taint. 'Known-world fiction' is admittedly clumsy, but it does the job.

idea-as-hero stories

In most known-world stories the focal pint of the story is the main character, but in many science fiction stories and some fantasy stories the focus shifts to the novum of the story. Kingsley Amis popularised the term 'idea-as-hero story' in order to discuss the distinctive features of works of this kind.

info-dumping

The central problem faced by writers of imaginative fiction is explaining to the reader exactly how the world within the text differs from the known world. Some critics use 'info-dumping' as an insult aimed at crude and unsatisfactory ways of tackling this problem but I have used it to refer to any process by which necessary background information is incorporated into a story.

novum

The central notion on which the plot of a fantasy or science fiction story pivots. Some critics prefer 'motif', especially when writing about fantasy; others think 'idea' is perfectly adequate, especially when writing about science fiction. 'Novum' was popularised by the critic Darko Suvin with specific reference to science fiction but I have adopted it for general use. See also idea-as-hero stories.

planetary romance

An action-adventure story set on an alien planet (usually, nowadays, a planet orbiting a distant star). Most planetary romances are, in effect, science-fictional versions of secondary-world fantasies.

plot coupons

A derisory term coined by Nick Lowe to describe the magical devices and items of information which characters in many quest fantasies must collect in order to make ready for their climactic confrontations. Alfred Hitchcock used to refer to the similar items which provided traction for the plots of his films as 'McGuffins'.

secondary worlds

Worlds which 'replace' the Earth in fantasy stories, usually differing from it in matters of geography and ecology but not in terms of physical conditions like gravity and atmospheric composition.

sense of wonder

A key aspect of the reader's response to many science fiction and some fantasy stories. The awakening of a sense of wonder at the size, complexity and strangeness of the universe is what draws many young readers to imaginative fiction and turns some of them into virtual addicts.

shared worlds

Imaginary worlds which are use by more than one author. Some are designed in advance of use for anthologies of stories by many hands; others are the invention of a single author which become so popular that they are opened up to use by other writers in order to exploit their potential profitability. Writers commissioned by publishers to produce stories set in other people's fictional worlds are sometimes described by unsympathetic critics as 'sharecroppers'.

SUGGESTIONS FOR FURTHER READING

John Clute and Peter Nicholls, eds., *The Encyclopedia of Science Fiction*, Orbit, 1993.

John Clute and John Grant, eds., *The Encyclopedia of Fantasy*, Orbit, 1997.

These invaluable reference books have articles on all the various themes and motifs employed in fantasy and science fiction. It is always a good idea, if you intend working with a particular idea or mythical entity, to have some knowledge of what has been done with it before. Research of this kind may also allow you to identify things which have not previously been tried, and which might therefore offer interesting possibilities.

Samuel R. Delany, *The Jewel-Hinged Jaw: Notes on the Language of Science Fiction*, Dragon Press, 1977; *Starboard Wine: More Notes on the Language of Science Fiction*, Dragon Press, 1984.

Challenging essays on the art of science fiction; the first volume includes 'Thickening the Plot' and 'About 5,750 Words', which were important landmarks in the linguistic analysis of science fiction.

Colin Greenland, *Michael Moorcock: Death is no Obstacle*, Savoy, 1992.

A collection of interviews, all of which are concerned with Moorcock's writing methods, objectives and sources of inspiration, adding up to an unusually thoroughgoing analysis.

Maxim Jakubowski and Edward James, *The Profession of Science Fiction*, Macmillan, 1992

The academic journal *Foundation* – currently edited by Edward James, who is professor of Medieval Studies at the University of Reading – has a regular feature in which writers discuss their work and its motivation. This collection reprints sixteen of them; the journal has published well over fifty and it is possible that more collections will appear in future.

Diana Wynne Jones, *The Tough Guide to Fantasyland*, Gollancz, 1995.

Another invaluable, though much less earnest, reference book which offers a blisteringly sarcastic account of all the newly hatched clichés of genre fantasy. You can use it cynically, albeit with gritted teeth, or you can use it as a directory of moves best avoided, according to your taste.

Ursula K. le Guin, *The Language of the Night: Essays on Fantasy and Science Fiction*, Women's Press, 1989.

The revised British edition of a collection first published in the USA by Putnam in 1979. It includes such classic reflections on the artistry of fantasy and science fiction as 'Dreams Must Explain Themselves', 'From Elfland to Poughkeepsie' and 'Science Fiction and Mrs Brown'.

The New York Review of Science Fiction, published monthly by Dragon Press, PO Box 78, Pleasantville, New York, NY 10570. UK subscriptions $44 per year.

A critical journal which often includes articles on the art and craft of writing, including some notable essays by Samuel R. Delany. My own essays on the subject, including the Pioneer Award-winning 'How Should a Science Fiction Story End?' usually appear in its pages.

J. R. R. Tolkien, 'On Fairy Stories' in *Tree and Leaf*, Unwin, 1964.

A classic essay on the psychological functions of fantasy, invaluable to an understanding of the way such stories work and their appeal to the audience.

Nancy Willard, *Telling Time: Angels, Ancestors, and Stories*, Harcourt Brace, 1993.

An excellent collection by a highly respected writer and teacher of creative writing; it contains some very fine essays on the art and craft of writing, with particular reference to the use of fantastic devices.

J. N. Williamson, ed., *How to Write Tales of Horror, Fantasy and Science Fiction*, Robinson, 1990.

The British edition of an anthology first issued by Writer's Digest Books in the USA in 1987. It has an introduction by Robert Bloch and twenty-two essays by writers of various vocation, including Ray Bradbury, Dean R. Koontz and Ramsey Campbell.

Robin Scott Wilson, ed., *Clarion*, Signet, 1971; *Clarion II*, Signet, 1972; *Those Who Can: A Science Fiction Reader*, Mentor, 1973.

Three anthologies mingling fiction and essays, early product of the annual Clarion workshops which have now been running in the USA for nearly thirty years. Students attend for six weeks, with pairs of professional tutors teaching a week at a time. The third volume is particularly useful because the essays consist of elaborate dissections by the authors of their exemplary stories.

The Year's Best Fantasy and Horror edited by Ellen Datlow and Terri Windling, and *The Year's Best Science Fiction* edited by Gardner Dozois, issued annually by St Martin's Press.

Two huge annual anthologies, each of which also includes an elaborate introductory 'summation' of the year's events and publications, with a perceptive running commentary on the progress of the various fields. The three editors are the best in the business – Dozois also edits *Asimov's Science Fiction*, Datlow edits fiction for *Omni On-Line* as well as being a prolific anthologist, solo and in collaboration with Windling – and they perform their Herculean tasks with magnificent dedication. The books are invaluable to writers wishing to keep track of the fantasy and science fiction marketplace.

INDEX